P9-DGE-497

Tenth printing — 348,000 copies
© Saint Joseph's Oratory

Legal Deposit — 2nd quarter, 1988
Bibliothèque nationale du Québec
National Library of Canada

ISBN 2-920067-06-0

Printed in Canada

HENRI-PAUL BERGERON, C.S.C.

BROTHER ANDRÉ, C.S.C.
THE WONDER MAN
OF MOUNT ROYAL

(Revised Edition)

Translated from the French

by

Rev. Real Boudreau, C.S.C.

Saint Joseph's Oratory
3800 Queen Mary Road
Montreal, Canada H3V 1H6

ACKNOWLEDGMENT

The author wishes to acknowledge his indebtedness to those who contributed in the work of translating this book, and especially to Reverend Sister Mary of Saint Hilda, C.S.C., of Saint-Laurent, Quebec, who revised this translation and greatly helped in making it more faithful and idiomatic, so far as time and circumstances permitted; and to Reverend Mother Mary of St. Eleanore, C.S.C., of St. Mary's College, Holy Cross, Indiana, who also revised the translation and the proofs.

BEHOLD, THE DREAMER COMETH

Beautiful upon the mountain were your feet, dear Brother André, bringing good tidings and preaching peace and showing forth goodness. Beautiful was your voice, the voice of the watchman, praising the goodness of God, Who comforts His people and sends His salvation to the ends of the earth.

You, who loved to call yourself Saint Joseph's little dog, would likely answer me with a characteristic twinkle in your eye: "Little dogs have noisy barks." But, oh, how beautiful was your voice when suffering washed its maimed and broken souls and bodies in an unending tide up the slope of the mountain to hear your words of healing, and how beautiful were your hands that lifted up those whom life had hurt so grievously and made them whole again!

In the long ago, Brother André, your father and mine in God, Basil Moreau, dreamed of a great international shrine to Saint Joseph. He dreamed also, as a father will, of good and great children and so he bade us ask Saint Joseph every morning to bless our Community and to "bring to it subjects who will glorify God." And Saint Joseph brought us you. We could not have dreamed of such an answer to this prayer, said so often sleepily and distractedly.

This little note of mine, dear Brother André, is to thank you for letting me visit you one time in your small Bureau and ask you something which you said Saint Joseph would take care of; it is to thank you for other favors, and especially for letting me edit this book.

This book surely will please you, Brother André, because it glorifies God in showing the wonders He wrought in your poor little self for the honor of His Foster-Father. It is a lovely book, a perfect biography (it even has a chapter on your imperfections) and so it will win its way into countless hearts. Though it is comforting to us sinners to know you had some imperfections, we but admire you the more because of your bottomless humility and contrition. You did not compare your holiness with our lack of it and hence make light of your faults. You compared your faults with God's holiness. This was your dream, to become perfect as also your Heavenly Father is perfect. We who love you believe that your angel of death came only to tell you that your dream came true.

The dream Saint Joseph put into your heart to build him a shrine where he could be a protecting father to the poor suffering ones of Christ also came true. Beautiful was your heart for harboring that dream and working and suffering for it through all the years. Men laughed at you and scorned you and calumniated you for that dream, but you kept it alive in your heart and toiled on for its fulfilment. The dream could not live on except in your heart, dear little Brother André, and so now your heart remains there in the midst of all the faith and the wonder and the glory, to treasure down the long years its dream come true.

SISTER MARY ELEANORE, C.S.C.

CONTENTS

INTRODUCTORY NOTE

In conformity with the decrees of the Roman Pontiffs, and especially those of Pope Urban VIII, concerning the beatification of the servants of God and the canonization of saints, we declare that the words "saint, sanctity, miracle, etc." contained in this biography are designations which stand for our personal impressions as well as those of the immediate witnesses to the story we are relating, and are not meant to anticipate the judgments of the Church, whose most humble and most submissive sons we are.

NOTE OF TRANSLATOR

We have throughout translated literally the French word *saint*, which in that language has wider connotation than usual in ours, including any holy person, even if not canonized.

I

MOTHER AND CHILD

THE humble village of Saint-Grégoire d'Iberville, which lies east of Montreal on a plain broken by isolated hills, has the honor of being the birthplace of Brother André. Its residents point with pride to a plot of ground at the crossroads leading to Saint-Grégoire and Marieville, saying:

"Here stood Brother André's first home."

Nothing now remains of this home, and only a broken-down fence and an old stunted elm mark its site. A rugged mountain, close by, like a mighty monster keeps guard above the birthplace of our saint.

In the calm peace of a cool October afternoon, within sight of Brother André's one-time home, I sat and mused. Nature was plunged in deep silence; the whole chorus of life that had chirped and sung during the radiant summer was heard no more. Everywhere the dying autumn splashed against the dark background of the green pines and firs on the hills, the brown and yellow of the beech, the dark purple of the ash tree, the orange of the saffron, and the brilliant scarlet of the maple.

While I was dreaming in this scenic beauty, the church bell pealed forth joyously, to announce the birth of a Christian; and at the sound, my imagination carried me back to a similar moment in the long ago.

BROTHER ANDRÉ, C.S.C.

It was August 10, 1845. From the belfry of a small church fashioned from Canadian field stones, a shrill bell announced that a humble procession was approaching the baptismal font. The curious villagers took note that Isaac Bessette was bringing his sixth child to the church for the Sacrament.

The child had been christened at the moment of his birth for fear that he might not live. On this, the following day, the ritual was completed at the church with conditional Baptism by the pastor who, while performing the ceremony, was probably thinking that this delicate infant would not be long for this world. The parish register shows the following record:

"On August 10, 1845, we, the undersigned, have baptized conditionally Alfred, born the previous day, of the lawful wedlock of Isaac Bessette, carpenter, and of Clothilde Foisy, of this parish. The godfather is Edouard Bessette and the godmother Josephine Foisy, uncle and aunt of the child, who, like the father, declare themselves unable to sign."

P. A. Sylvestre, *Pastor*.

Thanks to the mother's loving care, the child lived, but remained delicate throughout his life.

The parents had been married at Saint-Matthias, September 27, 1831. The father, like Saint Joseph, a carpenter and wheelwright, frequently moved from one village to another, as may be seen from the baptismal certificates of his numerous children.

Brother André, being made a Christian in his cradle, did not become saintly after a sudden conversion in the manner of Saint Paul, Saint Augustine, or Père de Fou-

[10]

cauld; and yet his spotless soul, in its expansion under God's watchful care, creates an interest just as fascinating though not as striking as did the souls of these great converts. Born of Canadian stock with its distinctly Catholic and French tradition, he is a genuine representative of his race.

His holiness took its source in the heart of his mother, who was intent on making him from his very cradle an heir to Heaven. Virtuous, meek, hard-working, the mother of the little Alfred proved herself an ideal Christian parent. At the knee of this illiterate woman of the people, he learned to lisp the names of Jesus, Mary and Joseph along with those of Papa and Mamma, and thus came to associate in his childish mind the love of his dear ones on earth with the love of the Heavenly Family.

God gives divine grace in the Sacrament of Baptism; the parents have the duty of cultivating a spiritual mentality in their children in their earliest years, for the soul of a child is as wax to receive and as bronze to retain the first impressions of childhood. Destinies are almost as a rule shaped at the knees of a mother.

It is pleasant to picture the home life in that isolated cottage on its bit of land, noisy with the clamor of six young children. The family remained at Saint-Grégoire for three years; but as each succeeding year brought with it another mouth to feed, the father was no longer able to provide for their wants. Hence, he resolved to leave this humble home and to take up residence in the little town of Farnham. There for two years he carried on the trade of wheelwright, until he met with accidental death while felling a tree in the woods. His desolate wife was thus left as the sole provider for their ten children.

Alfred had only a faint remembrance of his father; but he retained a vivid picture of his mother and loved to speak of her: "Because I was sickly, my mother always showed me a deeper affection than she showed the others. She used to kiss me repeatedly and often gave me little dainties. During the family evening prayer I used to kneel beside her and follow the Rosary on her beads. My mother was always smiling—such a lovely smile! Even since her death she often smiles at me. Sometimes I see her looking at me and loving me though she utters not a word. I seldom pray for my mother, but I often pray to her."

Under the guidance of his beloved mother his childish soul expanded freely. His piety was immediately remarkable. To those who in later years teased one of his sisters by insinuating that, after all, her brother was not such a great saint and that he had been in his youth a good-for-nothing, she made retort:

"You would not say that if you had known him in his early years. He used to spend endless hours praying in the church in Farnham."

During the four years succeeding the father's death, the mother was able to provide for the needs of her family; but at length, weakened by privation and nightly toil, consumed by the ravages of tuberculosis and slowly wasting away, she was forced to seek refuge with her sister, Madame Timothée Nadeau, who lived at Saint-Césaire. Only Alfred accompanied her, the rest of the family being dispersed among charitable relatives.

Comforted by the care of her sister and of her loving little son, the mother lingered for two years. When the end came, the children were brought to her bedside, and on November 10, 1857, she bade them final adieu. With the lucidity of thought customary to the dying tuberculous sufferer, she was able to say to her children:

"My dear ones, it is now six years since your father left you for Heaven. The good God wishes me also to leave you. Pray for me. Do not forget the grave of your father. Let my body rest beside his in the cemetery at Farnham.

From Heaven I shall watch over you."

Alfred shared in the distress of his dear mother over leaving her numerous children whose little hands still clung to hers. All his life long he kept a vivid remembrance of the deathbed of his grief-stricken mother. These separations of his childhood rent his soul with sorrow, detaching him from fleeting worldly pleasures and enkindling within him a thirst for loving self-sacrifice.

A mother's greatest concern is the future of her children, for she knows that these little ones whose coming among us entails many tears and sacrifices, bear within them the seed of eternal life. At the hour of death, in the ecstatic encounter with the Lord, little Alfred's mother must have said:

"I am but a poor woman, but through my humble efforts I have at least presented Thee with ten worshippers in whose hearts I have inculcated love for Thee in so far as my ignorance, my hard toil, and the shortness of my days on earth have allowed me. Lord, they are Thine; take care of them."

It is easy to imagine the answer: "These children will be your jewels in Heaven. There you will behold your Alfred, surrounded by the souls he will have won by his prayers and his tears, and the many sinners he will have drawn back to God by his example."

After the funeral the weeping orphans were again separated. Alfred returned to his aunt, whose physical appearance and character kept him reminded of his dead mother. His uncle hid under a stern exterior a very compassionate heart. Alfred was always greatly attached to his foster-parents, and certain extracts from his letters to them after his entry into the religious life manifest his lively affection for them:

"Though I have found happiness in the state of life which I have embraced, my dear uncle and aunt, I have not forgotten my benefactors. If, my kind uncle, I have put off too long my answer to your letter, it was only that I might write you for your patronal feast. As there is a general family custom of presenting a bouquet to the father on this day, I ask myself what more precious and sweet-smelling bouquet could I give you than my gratitude to you for your many benefits, what richer bouquet could I offer than the remembrance of all your solicitude and care for me."

Generous but also robust and hard-working, Timothée Nadeau intended to make of his own children, and of his adopted son as well, sturdy fellows able to earn a good living. The sensitive Alfred could not but miss the attentions that his mother had lavished on him. Later, he admitted in a confidential way and with his exquisite charity: "My uncle was a strong man and he thought everyone else as robust as himself."

It is easy to imagine the rugged peasant saying to the inconsolable orphan: "You have cried enough now. You are twelve years old and big enough to look out for yourself. When I was your age I ploughed the fields and earned my living. You must manage to get a livelihood, for we are not wealthy. As neither your health nor your ability permits you to go to school, I will have you begin your apprenticeship as a shoemaker."

Alfred acquiesced willingly; in fact, all his life long he was to be engaged willingly in hard labor. Not only did he have but little strength, but he always overused what resources he had. One can easily imagine the courageous little lad setting to work with intense activity, bending all day long over the thick hide from which he was making sturdy shoes. Now and then he would prick himself with the awl or strike his finger with the hammer. Besides, he was tortured by those severe pains in the stomach that were to torment him all his life.

From his own experience he learned to have compassion on the suffering and the hard-working. Later on, recalling the time when, as a pale and sickly youth, he had been tied down to his wearisome trade, he confessed that his labor was beyond his strength: "You know, working in a cobbler's shop almost on all fours and hammering away all day long is not an aid to one's digestion."

About that time, young Alfred made his First Holy Communion in Saint-Césaire's church. Fervent indeed must have been his first meeting with Jesus in the Blessed Sacrament, for the teachings of his pious mother were still vivid in his mind, and all his lifelong he was a devoted lover of the Holy Eucharist.

Father Provençal, the parish priest and a devout client of Saint Joseph, prepared the boy for the great moment. No one could doubt Alfred's fidelity in following the cate- chetical instruction or in listening to the narratives of the Gospel. He had already often thought of Saint Joseph watching over the Child Jesus and he had made up his mind to imitate this saintly Workman, for he also was to watch over the Infant God Whom he carried at all times in his soul by divine grace and Whom he received with such deep piety in Holy Communion.

A First Communion picture lets us see the appearance of the boy at that time. His pale, delicate face is lit by brilliant dark eyes, one a bit smaller than the other. His expression is a mixture of gentle introspection and eager energy.

One evening Alfred was very ill. Madame Nadeau, while helping him into bed, noticed that he grimaced uncontrollably with pain while she undressed him, and asked:

"What is that thing under your shirt?"

"Oh, nothing much."

"Let me see, my child."

She uncovered a barbed leather cincture. Then she said: "But this is very foolish. With your miserable health, you should do sensible penance."

"Dear aunt, it was a sacrifice I promised to make. Forgive me. I shall take it off." Filled with admiration, she took him in her arms and kissed him. Some time later, she took from him an iron chain he was wearing round his waist. To her reproaches the child replied:

"I shall take it off." True, he took it off, but he used his wit to find one new kind of penance after another. His adopted brothers mocked him for his penances and reported to the mother:

"Alfred does not sleep in the bed; he sleeps on the floor. We saw him."

"Is it true, Alfred?" When he nodded his head without saying a word, she said: "You will make yourself sick. Do not do that again."

His little cousins, with the mercilessness characteristic of their age, liked to play pranks and then blame him for them. When alone, he often shed tears; but these trials and labors were God's way of preparing the boy for his future mission.

That he might the better serve as a model for the working classes, Divine Providence ordained that he should work at various trades. After eking out a scanty living as an apprentice shoemaker, he gave up this occupation to work in a baker's shop.

On April 5, 1860, Timothée Nadeau joined the "gold rush" to California with hundreds of other Canadians in a migration caused by the inability of the government at the time to protect and encourage the farmers, especially of the Quebec region. He had settled his family in Farnham, and Alfred, then aged fifteen, left to himself, became a hand on the Ouimet farm, on the outskirts of the village.

Though the boy was cheerful, obliging, and hard-working, he was, unlike most boys, fonder of prayer than of play. In his spare time during the usual hours of rest or on rainy days, he recited his Rosary and dreamed about his beloved mother.

The pastor of Saint-Césaire had taught the boy to give special honor to Saint Joseph and now he became accustomed to converse with this great Saint. His devotion soon developed into an ardent love which made his whole life an unceasing effort to imitate the Model of the laborer. In Saint Joseph he found the ideal he strove to reproduce and the friend who guided him to sanctity.

Even in those early years, the spiritual drive of Alfred's whole life began to appear in his two great devotions. By the radiance of example Saint Joseph caused the interior life of his young apostle to flower into a tender love of Jesus Crucified, a love modeled on and united to that of the Foster-Father of the Saviour. In the ascent towards God, Alfred progressed steadily without the least resistance to grace and always with heroic generosity.

His employer, Mr. Ouimet, bought a crucifix at an auction. He noticed the boy fairly devouring it with his eyes, and hence he asked: "Would you care to have it?"

"Oh, yes, indeed I would, sir."

The gift was bestowed. Shortly after, noticing that Alfred lingered in the barn every evening after the long day's toil, the farmer went to find him one evening and discovered him kneeling before the crucifix, which he had fastened to a beam.

Soon afterwards, the boy was noticed to be somewhat incapacitated in his work. Upon examination, the cause of his trouble was discovered: he was wearing a tight iron chain round his waist.

At that time occurred an incident which clearly shows his angelic purity. During an evening party he observed

[17]

that those present were becoming too boisterous. Despite
sarcastic comments, he soon withdrew quietly. On his way
home, while he was passing over a small bridge, he heard
an unusual murmuring sound different from that of the
brook babbling over its stony bed. Immediately the
thought of his mother flashed into his mind, and he exclaimed: "Dear Mother, if this sound be to warn me not
to return to that place, let me hear it again." Again the
sound rose distinctly to his ears.

Without passing judgment on the value of this omen,
we can at least conclude from the incident how the
remembrance of his beloved mother saved him from peril
while he was young and left to himself.

When about fifteen years of age, Alfred left Saint-
Césaire for Farnham. There, he tried first to become a
blacksmith, and in later years delighted in telling laborers
who complained of their hardships how he used to shoe
horses and work iron.

He was, however, soon compelled to leave this occupation, which was beyond his strength. He next found
employment with Father Springer, the parish priest at
Farnham; and in this new occupation, which brought him
close to the altar, he had the opportunity of giving free
rein to his piety.

When Alfred was twenty years old, he followed the
example of hundreds of other young French Canadians,
leaving his native province of Quebec to seek employment
in New England. It was in the designs of God that he came
to the United States, the better to be put personally to the
test, and the more readily in the future to spread the
devotion to Saint Joseph. Later on, in fact, the work of
Brother André was propagated even more widely in the

United States than in Canada.

At the time Alfred, though twenty years old, seemed on account of his small stature and his thin, pallid face, no more than sixteen. His modest and recollected countenance glowed with the fire of divine love burning in his heart. He had long since grown accustomed to the practice of praying unceasingly during his work and of conversing with his favorite Saint, the Workman of Nazareth.

For three years Alfred lived in the United States, working now on a farm, now in a factory. He worked successively in mills in the cities of Moosup, Hartford, and Phoenix. His precarious health forced him to alternate between the more remunerative work of the cities and the more healthful work of the country. Never discouraged, he struggled for his living, trying as much as possible to imitate the toilsome and prayerful life of his patron Saint. His companions at work were greatly astonished at seeing him devote nearly all his spare time to prayer.

When speaking of those days of exile, he liked to recount a dream that seemed to have some relation to his vocation. The life of Brother André affords a striking resemblance to that of Saint Joseph. So far as we know, there were hardly any ecstasies or other extraordinary phenomena, but there were a number of marvellous dreams. In this particular dream Alfred was working in the field and, being very tired, he leaned on his rake, and said to Saint Joseph: "Where shall I die?" At that moment there loomed before his eyes a large stone building such as he had not seen before. The remembrance of this incident remained deeply impressed in his memory. Many years later he realized this dream picture to be an exact replica of Notre Dame College in Montreal. Though he did not actually die in that building, he spent forty years of his religious life there, and there also he laid the foundation of his lifework, the Oratory of Saint Joseph.

II

VOCATION

Alfred Bessette was twenty-three years of age when he returned to his native land to live with relatives in the village of Sutton, near the American border. While at Farnham and in the United States, he had kept up a friendly correspondence with Father Provençal, a noble character whom Divine Providence had designed to guide him. A Brother of Holy Cross, who was indebted to this holy priest for his vocation, paid him the following tribute:

"Father Provençal was a saint. All his parishioners were very fond of him, and the words engraved on his tomb near the church sum up his wonderful career: 'He was kind. He loved us.'"

Father Provençal was a pastor beloved by all and filled with solicitude for his flock. He used to carry his hat in his hand when he went out because of the large number of salutations he had to exchange with the villagers, who would hasten to surround him whenever he appeared.

Sometimes Alfred went to Saint-Césaire and spent a few days at the rectory. Referring to his devotion to Saint Joseph, he declared: "When Father Provençal needed my services, he always looked for me in the church at the foot of Saint Joseph's statue."

The boy had been left to himself from childhood, and yet, after three years of adventurous life in the United

States, where it was at that time easy for a young stranger to lose the Faith, he came home as pious, as ignorant of worldly pleasures as before his departure from Canada.

The pastor of Saint-Césaire was most solicitous about the education of youth. In 1869 he had a commercial college built and gave over its direction to the religious of Holy Cross. At the time of Alfred's visit to the parish priest, six Brothers lived in the new boarding school, which was opposite the rectory. One day Father Provençal asked Alfred:

"Have you ever thought of becoming a religious and living all your life in a house where there is a chapel in which you could assist at holy Mass and receive Holy Communion daily?"

"But don't you know, Father, that I cannot write or even read?"

"What does that matter? Not all religious are teachers. In a Congregation like the one that has come here, there are Brothers who devote themselves to manual labor. Would you not like to become a religious of Holy Cross?"

"Do you really think I have a vocation?"

"I am convinced of it, my son. Pray to God that He may enlighten you."

"Many thanks, Father. I shall think it over."

Alfred examined the garb of these religious: their black habit similar to a priest's cassock, their Roman collar, their long woolen cincture with a tassel at the ends, and their plain wooden cross and medal of Saint Joseph. He discussed with them their manner of living and their special devotion to the Patriarch of Nazareth.

The religious, however, did not urge him to enter the novitiate, for they were well aware of his delicate health, though they willingly gave him whatever information he desired. The Congregation of Holy Cross is composed of two distinct elements, the Fathers and the Brothers, representing the intimate union existing between Jesus and His Foster-Father. The Community was founded in Le Mans, France, by a holy priest, Father Basil Moreau, and at the request of Bishop Bourget of Montreal, a group of the religious were sent to Canada in 1847. By 1870, the Congregation of Holy Cross had many flourishing institutions. Among the Brothers there is a group who devote themselves to manual work in imitation of the life of Saint Joseph, their Patron. Living in close union with God, many of these, the lay-Brothers, have sanctified themselves in their obscure task of serving their fellow members. Less exposed to temptations of pride and freed from the all-absorbing solicitude of the preacher or the teacher, they find their work easily conducive to meditation on the life of the Master.

Alfred Bessette was delighted at the prospect of such happiness. The religious life corresponded to the most secret yearnings of his vagrant youth. His urge for moving from one house, one farm, or one factory to another, betrayed his restless longing to find a way of life in which he could do more directly for God. He now realized that his distaste for the world and the mysterious uneasiness which harassed him in his prayers were indications of a divine call to the religious state, and he burned with desire to embrace his vocation.

In early autumn of the year 1870 he set out for Montreal. Scarcely two months earlier, the religious of Holy Cross had transferred their novitiate from Saint-Laurent to a new establishment, opened the preceding year at Côte-des-Neiges. The Bellevue Hotel, a long, wooden structure on the western slope of Mount Royal, designed in a plain architectural pattern with pediment and four columns,

BROTHER ANDRÉ, C.S.C.

had been converted into a combined college and novitiate.
Alfred Bessette was received with open arms by Father
Julien Gastineau, who held the twofold office of president
of the college and master of novices. A letter from the
pastor of Saint-Césaire had already informed him about
the newcomer:

"I am sending a saint to your Congregation."

This testimonial from the priest, who had known the
boy from infancy, was true in the full sense of the word.
Alfred's was not a heart tarnished and heavy with the
pleasures of the world, a mind surrendered to earthly
allure; rather, he brought to the religious life a heart
desirous of attaining the highest supernatural ideal and
already accustomed to the only delights which Jesus be-
stows on His privileged ones: trials, scourges, crosses. His
soul was filled with the love of God, which swept him to
ever higher levels.

One can easily imagine the difficulties with which a
young man of twenty-five, who had long been his own
master, had to cope in complying with the demands of
religious discipline. At the very beginning, however, he
showed himself a model of obedience, self-sacrifice, and
piety. On December 27, 1870, after some weeks of trial,
work and prayer by way of preparation, he received the
religious habit, in that always impressive ceremony in
which the young postulant gives himself to God. The priest
who presided over the ritual, addressing him thus: "Alfred
Bessette, henceforth thy name will be Brother André," a
name chosen as a mark of gratitude toward Father André
Provençal, was doubtless far from suspecting that the
young man before him was to become the founder of such
a great work as the Oratory of Saint Joseph, and was
destined to realize through his efforts the hope expressed
by the Curé of Ars:

"The Congregation of Holy Cross is destined after many

[24]

trials to perform great works."

That very year Pope Pius IX declared Saint Joseph the Patron Saint of the Universal Church.

In the solitude of the novitiate Brother André set himself sedulously to reproduce in his own life the teachings of Christ and to conform to the ideal set forth in the Gospel. That assiduous conformity in the most minute details of his life with the life of his Divine Exemplar was his chief concern during this year spent in the solitary retreat that initiates into the religious life. In the attainment of virtue he was assisted greatly by Father Gastineau, in whom he found an experienced and capable counsellor.

★

★ ★

In the course of the following year, the religious at Saint-Laurent College, being too few in number longer to meet all the demands of the institution, requested the help of the novices. These, therefore, were brought to live in "the white house," an old building with white-washed walls behind the college. Father Gastineau remained as superior of Côte-des-Neiges, and Father Guy became master of novices.

Brother André was made linen keeper and infirmarian, and had also the task of keeping the corridors neat and clean. Though such a novitiate was necessarily wanting in organization, Brother André did not cease to progress in sanctity. He was greatly assisted by a spiritual director of rare merit, Father Hupier, who was held in such high esteem by all that, when he died two years later, his parishioners violently opposed the transfer of his remains to Montreal. Brother André held his memory in great veneration.

Though in the novitiate Brother André found a director eminently qualified to offer him spiritual guidance, throughout the rest of his life he was practically deprived of such help. Like a master sculptor who is jealous of his own glory in producing a masterpiece and allows his pupils only to rough-hew, the Holy Ghost reserves the moulding of saints in great part to Himself. The Little Flower, for example, complained that she could never find a true director. Brother André, revering his spiritual father as a saint, declared one day:

"Father Hupier appeared to me in a dream, and I asked him which prayer is the most pleasing to the good God. He recited the Our Father three times and then added, 'You must often repeat, "Thy will be done." ' From this I concluded that I should have to undergo great trials."

To a religious to whom, contrary to his custom, he had been giving his confidence, he began thus to relate another dream:

"Saint Frances of Rome has given me a good piece of advice——"

Then seeing that someone was jotting down his words in a notebook, he stopped for fear of wounding humility.

The Our Father, composed by Our Lord Himself, is indeed the most beautiful of prayers, and the repetition of the words, "Thy will be done," was really necessary for Brother André, for throughout his life he had to endure many difficult trials.

After a few months spent in the novitiate, he saw his vocation endangered by the fact that his superiors feared he would be of but little use to the Community because of his poor health and hence decided to dismiss him. A long time afterwards Brother André related how, being in the greatest distress, he had at that time thrown himself at the feet of Bishop Bourget on the occasion when the prelate had come to visit the religious at Saint-Laurent. The young novice, pale and sickly, somehow mastered his timidity and knocked at the Bishop's door. The prelate, an old man with long white hair and the emaciated features of an ascetic, yet erect despite his seventy-two years, welcomed the Brother with kind and fatherly words:

"What can I do for you, my son?"

The novice, prostrate at the Bishop's feet, with clasped hands and tearful eyes filled with anxious expectation, confided that his beautiful dream of becoming a religious had been frustrated, and that he was to be dismissed because of his lack of health. He avowed his love of God and his desire to serve Him in the most humble occupations.

"Do not fear, my dear son, you will be allowed to make your religious profession."

Perhaps some presentiment of the future work of this novice had entered the Bishop's mind when he looked down into the pleading, wistful face of the Brother. He was himself beset with a strong desire for honoring Saint Joseph, a project which he had not yet realized and of which he had already written these prophetic words:

"We must have a church specially dedicated to his cult in which he may receive daily the public homage worthy of his eminent virtues. . . . We wish to consecrate all our strength and the rest of our life to making him honored in such a church, establishing there a place of pilgrimage where the people will come to him."

By the mysterious guidance of Divine Providence, the Bishop himself had gone to France in 1836, to ask Father Moreau to send a few religious to his diocese. The two godly men made a strange bargain: the founder of the Congregation of Holy Cross gave the Bishop nine of his subjects for Canada, and the prelate, as a token of gratitude, gave Father Moreau a precious relic which he had brought from Rome, the body of a four-year-old martyr who had been put to death during the early persecutions. Perhaps the Bishop foresaw that the religious family which he had purchased with the remains of a saint would prepare the chosen one of God, the founder of the great shrine dedicated to Saint Joseph.

The novice left the Bishop, cheered and entirely consoled by so much kindness. Later, when relating this incident, he said:

"Ah, Bishop Bourget is now raised high in heavenly bliss. Pray to him often. Indeed, he is high in Heaven."

Owing perhaps to the intervention of the holy Bishop, the Father master of novices not long after whispered in the ear of Brother André: "Do not be worried or afraid. I shall see to it that you are admitted to your vows."

To justify himself, he declared: "If this young man becomes unable to work, he can at least pray well."

Before long, Brother André had the great happiness of making his first temporary vows. At the Community Mass, in the presence of the priest who held the Sacred Host above the ciborium just before Holy Communion, he read the prescribed form which he had written in his unskilled hand:

"I, Joseph Alfred Bessette, Brother André, unworthy though I am, relying nevertheless on the divine mercy and earnestly desiring to devote myself to the service of the adorable Trinity, make to Almighty God the vows of poverty, chastity and obedience, according to the sense of the rules and constitutions of this Congregation, in the presence of Our Lord Jesus Christ, of the Blessed Virgin Mary conceived without sin, of her worthy spouse Saint Joseph, and of all the heavenly court, promising to accept whatever employments it may please my superiors to entrust to me."

His vocation to the religious life was then accomplished. That of his mission as the apostle of Saint Joseph was beginning.

III

SOWING TIME

A T THE end of Brother André's novitiate he was appointed porter at Notre Dame College, where he had begun his religious life. Cheerful and obliging, he soon became accustomed to this his first appointment. He was to spend forty years of his life in this house, wherein about two hundred boys were entrusted to the care of a small number of religious. In his later years he used to say of this appointment:

"At the end of my novitiate, my superiors showed me the door and I stayed there for forty years—without leaving."

What had been the former Bellevue Hotel had given way to a large stone structure like the one he had seen in a dream before entering the Community. In 1881, the right wing of the college was built; in 1888, the central part and the chapel were constructed; and in 1890, the remainder of the building was completed.

The visitor may still see the porter's cell near the parlor, a small room hardly six feet square, dimly lighted by a little window. The furniture includes a wardrobe, a small desk, a bench along the wall, a chair, and on the bare walls are a crucifix and a picture of Saint Joseph. A thinly upholstered couch serves for a bed.

The religious in the house were very few in number.

Brother André, as his confrères, was overloaded with a multitude of occupations. As porter, he had to answer the doorbell and look for the religious and the students who were called to the parlor. He had to awaken the religious at five o'clock in the morning, knocking at each door and saying the traditional "*Benedicamus Domino*." During the day he rang the bell for the various exercises, always with that strict punctuality which distinguished him all his life. Besides his duties as porter, he kept the parlor and three corridors neat and clean, and went on errands to the town and took care of the mail. Every Monday and Saturday he drove to town with a horse and carriage for the students' laundry, which was done at the homes of their parents. In odd hours he served as barber and, while cutting the hair of the pupils, he tried to awaken in them devotion to Saint Joseph, "the father of the little Jesus." In the evening he prepared the altar breads, made cinctures for the religious, and did any other available jobs, spending himself with self-forgetful activity and untiring devotedness. The superior expressed a wish to have a lawn in front of the college, and Brother André immediately assumed this task, often laboring at it till late in the evening. He said of this work:

"Very late in the evening I used to carry from a distance of several yards the stones I had dug out of the ground in my few leisure moments during the day. It is amusing now to note that, to avoid too much fatigue and waste of time, I used two wheelbarrows. I would push one for about fifty yards and then return to get the other, thus resting myself and also saying my Rosary. Sometimes I was still working when the cock crew, and then I would go straightway to ring the bell to awaken the Community."

Such zeal can evidently be considered excessive; but the excellent intention was to fulfill as soon as he could the wish of his superior. That which appears strange to us in these later times is not at all out of order when we consider that the Community was then making its difficult beginning in Canada.

All these heroic sacrifices contributed to the sanctification of this humble servant of God. One is simply amazed at the amount of energy displayed by this little man, who could hardly digest a few mouthfuls of food. He was still tortured by severe pains in the stomach, but his health was the least of his concerns; he did his duty to the best of his ability and trusted all else to Divine Providence. His only food most of the time was a crust of bread dipped in milk and water. He ate at a corner of the table, alone and in haste, since his occupation as porter did not allow him to eat at the same time as the rest of the Community. Only a few of his confrères knew about these austerities, the superior not being among them. And yet Brother André never took advantage of his ill health to be relieved of any of his work.

In later years Brother André related these facts with his usual simplicity, not desiring sympathy for his sufferings, but trying to make clear that weakness does not prevent one with a good will from working: "During fifteen years I never asked the help of a confrère and I never refused anything which was asked of me. I accepted it all, and when I was unable to finish the work in the daytime, I did it at night."

At the age of forty-three he was exhausted from overwork. Toward the end of the summer, just before the opening of fall classes, the college physician one day found him washing the windows in the parlor. He warned Brother André that unless he took a complete rest, he would die within two months. The little Brother continued his work undisturbed. Some days later the doctor caught him again working as hard as ever. To his reproof Brother André retorted with a smile:

"If I die, my Community will be well rid of me."

Thus he, upon whom so many duties devolved, far from thinking himself indispensable, considered himself a burden to his Congregation. He was convinced that his vocation was such an inestimable grace that it could not be requited even by the most complete sacrifice of self. He liked to speak lightly of his labors, as, for example, when he once told some astonished Sisters:

"I had been scrubbing all night long, but this morning I received Holy Communion."

One day a lady who met him in the parlor said to him: "How different you look today, Brother André!"

"No wonder," he retorted, laughing; "I always change my clothes for Sunday."

In the midst of his many occupations he prayed incessantly. He liked to meditate on the sufferings of Our Saviour and to converse with Saint Joseph. He was always very regular in the performance of his religious exercises, which most of the time he had to make privately because of his duties. After the morning prayer and meditation, which he made with the Community, he used to hear holy Mass, kneeling on the floor at the back of the chapel close to the door so that he could hear the doorbell. There, like the publican in the Gospel, he remained, motionless and deeply devout.

Great was his joy when, during the day, a confrère would take his place at the door to free him for a short period. He would ask: "Will you please be kind enough to mind the door for me? I want to make a Holy Hour."

"Yes, provided you do not remain too long."

Brother André, altogether happy, would hasten to the chapel, where he would kneel on the floor at the entrance to the sanctuary. He had no notion of time when in the presence of his Beloved. Finally his substitute would come for him.

"Brother, you have been here praying for two hours.

That is surely enough."

"Oh, just five minutes more, please."

The other, unable to resist his pleading look, would go, but would have to return.

"Now I've been waiting more than fifteen minutes. I must go to teach my class."

With profuse apologies and thanks, the little Brother would reluctantly leave his prayer.

One evening, after a long day's work, he knocked timidly at the door of a confrère and then begged a great favor of him:

"I am dying with fatigue, and so I fear I shall fall asleep while saying my prayers. Will you kindly come and pray with me?"

The other, a young priest, consented. But the prayer lasted so long that he was exhausted and declared that he would never be caught again. The next time he was asked, he alleged a pressing duty and refused. Brother André had recourse to someone else. But soon everyone avoided the invitation, having heard from the victims of the long duration of the prayers.

Tired out as he was, especially on Wednesday and Saturday evenings when, after the usual day's work, he scrubbed the floor in the parlor, he performed his religious exercises in the chapel after the others had retired. There in the darkness he prayed and prayed until, overcome by fatigue, he fell asleep on his knees. Soon, however, he woke up and resumed his prayers, which he knew by heart. Sometimes this heroic struggle lasted till daybreak.

Because the souls of religious remain young, they are interested in the most insignificant facts. A trifling incident occurred which informed the whole Community about these nights spent in prayer. The porter one night fell sleep in the chapel, which was illuminated only by the le light of the sanctuary lamp. All at once, he started up out of his sleep. He saw a ray of light filtering through the small round window communicating with an empty room above the apse. Then he thought he heard a noise and was frightened. He hastened to go and knock at the door of a confrère.

"Come with me, Brother," he said, "there are some thieves above the chapel!"

The other religious hastily accompanied Brother André to the chapel, and after a careful investigation discovered that the lantern of the supposed marauders was only the freakish reflection of the moon creeping in through the window.

One of the confrères decided to lock the door in order to prevent Brother André from going into the chapel at night. Then he hid himself to witness the discomfiture of the little doorkeeper; but, to his amazement, he saw the latter entering the chapel without difficulty. When he related this strange fact to others, they laughed at what they considered his naïveté.

The pupils, with their keen discernment, soon detected the little tricks played on the porter, and made them the frequent subject of their conversation. With apparent guilelessness they began to ask their teachers various questions, their secret purpose being to find out who was for and who against Brother André. These boarding-school incidents of 1890 have been handed down to us by an eyewitness, then ten years old, who was attending the school as a day-pupil and was preparing for his First Holy Communion. Sometimes the porter gave letters to the boy to be posted and occasionally conversed with him. One day the boy asked Brother André:

"Where were you going last night? I saw you climbing up the mountain."

"I went to pray to Saint Joseph. It is so quiet there!"

"And you do go alone, Brother?"

"Yes, would you like to come with me?"

"Yes, I would very much, Brother."

"Then ask permission of your mother, and come and meet me after supper."

The boy, rejoicing, came at the appointed time. They climbed up by a narrow footpath till they reached a small clearing. Then they knelt near a tree.

"I have concealed a medal of Saint Joseph here. Let us pray that we may be able to buy this piece of land."

From that day on, they came regularly to the same spot. Brother André would tell the boy: "We will obtain this piece of land. Saint Joseph needs it."

Brother André could not be content with merely working hard, leading an exemplary life as a religious, and then saying after the day's toil: "I have done enough for Thee, O Lord, it is not for me, an ignorant man, to preach the love of God and propagate devotion to Saint Joseph." No, the little Brother knew more of love than that; he loved with all his soul so intensely that his love flowed from his own heart into the hearts of others. This workman can be a model for all Christians who comprehend their religion and wish to save the souls of others by the humble means within their power.

When he asked his confrères to unite with him in prayer, it was only a pretext to promote in them the great devotion with which God inspired him. One day the bursar said to him:

"Brother André, can you explain why it is that every time I put things in order in my office, I find my little statue of Saint Joseph turned towards the mountain?"

"It is because he wants to be honored there."

Brother André was always ready to do a kind act or give

a word of counsel. His countenance beamed with a geniality and a youthfulness of mind which attracted the pupils to him. Mischievous as all boys are, they sometimes took unfair advantage of his kindness, but they loved him. He spoke to them of the supernatural with a simplicity and a warmth of conviction that won them. The parents of the pupils also enjoyed talking with him, telling him their troubles and imploring his prayers, which they found very efficacious.

At this time he began his charitable work on behalf of the sick, to whom he was known as "good Brother André." His daily rounds to the post office gave him an opportunity of calling on the sick. On the occasion of these visits, he would give the suffering some of the oil that had been burned in front of the statue of Saint Joseph in the college chapel. The members of his Congregation paid no attention at the time to this original project, but the people among whom he visited began to venture timidly the idea:

"Brother André is a saint. He can heal the sick."

Thus far his confrères knew nothing about this power of the little Brother. One day when the porter intended to be away longer than usual, he got a young Brother to take his place. Unfortunately, while the substitute was absent for a few moments, a visitor arrived unexpectedly. On hearing the doorbell ring several times, the superior, Father Louage, an impetuous Frenchman born in the south of his country, came down from his office and made the whole house resound with the bell. The young Brother, much dismayed, soon appeared, and Brother André also came in at that very moment, to find the house in an uproar. The superior exclaimed:

"I am provincial, superior, bursar, and now I am expected to be doorkeeper! Kiss the floor, kiss the floor, kiss the floor, Brother André!" Without a word of self-defense, the little Brother performed the act of humility

This superior had a great reputation for virtue, for he was in truth endowed with a noble heart and was remarkable for his exactitude in observance of the rule. Though he had a very irascible temperament, his subjects loved him, for they knew he hid a paternal heart under his impetuous exterior, and they made him the object of many pleasant jibes. They styled Brother André the "lightning rod of the college," for on him fell the thunderbolts of Father Louage's displeasure.

Never did Brother André try to explain his conduct or to exonerate himself from accusations. His duties as porter often exposed him to receive reprimands from some of his confrères, such as:

"Instead of passing your time in prayers, you should be doing your duty. Why did you not call me to the parlor when someone came for me?"

The good Brother might have answered: "I went all through the college without finding you. If you stayed in your room when you should, this would not have happened. The superior told me not to summon anyone to the parlor under such circumstances."

Brother André, however, received the avalanche of scolding humbly, his head bowed as if he were indeed guilty, and without a word of self-defense. Those who saw this have said: "We marvelled at his sweetness and humility. In his place we should surely have defended ourselves. But he, never spoke a word."

It often happens that God permits the faults of others as a means of sanctification for His elect. Saint Teresa, who had much to suffer in her cloister, used to say:

"By whom can God sanctify us if not by those with whom we live?"

To the daily trials of the monastic life, to habitual mortifications such as sleeping on the bare floor, fastings, nights spent in work and prayer, putting up with the difficult young, Brother André added a multitude of sacrifices which he had been practicing since his childhood days. For illustration that one need not be over-delicate of self, he declared:

"During the winter nights I used to take baths in ice-cold water in the blacksmith's shop and sometimes I plunged naked into the snow behind the college."

These penances may have been means of fighting against the temptations with which the devil, who knew how much good Brother André was doing, assailed him. Soon, however, discouraged by vain efforts, Satan gave up his attacks of this kind and confined himself in peevish impotence to giving the little Brother a great deal of trouble physically, as he is wont to do with the saints. Many a narrative from Brother André has brought this to light.

Accustomed as he was to live always in the supernatural, he related the following fact, to prove how God in His goodness rewards the virtue of obedience, totally unconscious in his simplicity of the lustre it would give himself. As he often took care of the sick, healing them or preparing them to die, the people in the vicinity became accustomed to ask him to lay out their dead. One Sunday morning a boy called on Brother André to tell him that his grandfather, whom he had promised to prepare for burial, had just died.

"I will go about seven o'clock," answered the Brother, whom obedience retained at the college.

The boy went home, but his parents sent him back to tell Brother André: "You must come immediately; otherwise the corpse will become too rigid to be dressed."

"I cannot go now, so you will have to wait till evening. I am not allowed to leave the college on visiting days."

At supper time, having finished the day's work, Brother André went to the home of the dead man and found th

[38]

body still warm and flexible. He put the remains into the coffin without the least difficulty. Then, noticing that the head was somewhat inclined, he tried to put it into proper position, but found the operation very difficult, for at that moment the rigidity of death had set in.

On his return to the college he said his endless prayers and then retired to his room, which was isolated from those of his confrères, as they lived on the floor above. When he had entered his room he heard in the adjoining refectory a deafening noise as if glasses, cups, and plates were being knocked together and broken to pieces. He rushed into the dining-room and made a light. To his amazement he found that everything was in its proper place and nothing was broken.

This same strange sound occurred again on several occasions, and finally Brother André declared: "Every time I go to lay out a corpse, I hear that noise."

Sometimes also he saw a strange animal, a sort of huge black cat which seemed to cause the unusual noise. The presence of such a creature was inexplicable, and so he concluded: "The devil, enraged on account of my errands of mercy, is trying to frighten me."

There are doubtless many who, on reading these facts, can hardly refrain from smiling, being inclined to dismiss as legendary the intervention of the devil in the lives of the saints. It will be interesting for them to read the life of the Curé of Ars, to which that of Brother André has so many similarities, for they will find that the Evil One used to vent his anger in the same childish fashion against the Saint who was snatching from him so many souls. Oftentimes, the devil appeared to him under the form of an animal and produced a noise that was like the tearing of his curtains, sheets, and pillow-slips.

That Brother André endured such vexations many times may be inferred from confidences given by him on

various occasions. Thus did God's chosen one prepare himself for his great vocation by prayer, sufferings, and trials
of all kinds. This hidden life was the season of the sowing,
when he planted the seed that was to blossom during the
time of his public life as an apostle of Saint Joseph.

IV

THE OPENING BUD

B ROTHER ANDRÉ was thirty-four years old when the Saint of Lourdes, one year his senior, died. Bernadette's mission had long since been realized, and pilgrims were flocking to the rock of Massabielle, the sanctuary of the Immaculate Virgin. Through the mysterious ways of Providence, the apostle of Saint Joseph had to wait twenty-five years more before seeing his mission accomplished.

Bernadette, to carry out her purpose, had only to bear witness to the apparitions of the Blessed Virgin and then, when at last through many difficulties she had made her voice heard, she was able to retire into the seclusion of a convent.

In the case of Brother André, it was the miraculous power of working cures in the name of Saint Joseph that made it possible for him to fulfill his mission, which he followed closely to the very end of his life. For thirty-three years he watched over its development, being considered meantime in the public eye the faithful imitator of the Carpenter of Nazareth. Though from his earliest infancy Brother André had cherished a special devotion to his great friend Saint Joseph and had from the very beginning of his religious life labored by every means to spread the devotion, it was only when he was granted the extraordinary faculty of bestowing divine gifts that his mission began. What the apparitions of the Blessed Virgin were to the work of Bernadette, the power of miracles was for Brother André.

Little by little this power was made manifest, but those about him were slow to perceive it. The power of his intercession availed first among his confrères and the students. Some events which they did not at first perceive to be supernatural were nevertheless engraved on their memories and related afterwards.

The college bursar, a model religious, who shared with Brother André the dubious honor of being styled Father Louage's lightning-rod, had been confined to his bed for over a month because of an injury to his leg. Some days before the nineteenth of March he said to the porter:

"There is no improvement in my condition. I positively believe I shall not be able to go down to the chapel to celebrate the feast of Saint Joseph."

"Make the novena with me, have faith, and be assured you will be able to go to the chapel."

On the morning of the feast all the religious were astonished to see in their ranks the patient who had been seriously ill in bed the day before. After Mass, they were assured that there remained no trace whatever of the injury.

Brother André was no less solicitous for the pupils and, of these, the orphans were the first to receive the kind attentions and the devotedness of his compassionate heart. Those among them who were ill sometimes benefited by his powerful intercession.

In conversation with intimate friends, the little Brother, while recalling the beginning of his career at Notre Dame College, related the following incident. A pupil suffering from a malignant fever had been confined to bed in the infirmary for several days. During recreation, the porter called at the infirmary and said with a smile:

"What are you doing here, you lazy boy?"

"I am sick."

"Get up."

"The doctor ordered me to stay here."

"But you are not sick any more. Go on out for recreation."

The child, already feeling better, did not need to be told twice. He dressed and ran out to romp with his fellow pupils, much to the astonishment of the recreation-master. An inquiry was made, and Brother André was charged with imprudence and with interference in the functions of the infirmarian.

"But the boy is not sick," was his ready answer. "Have him examined."

The doctor examined the boy and found no trace of the sickness. Thoroughly puzzled, he came back several times that day and finally could not doubt the permanence of the cure.

An epidemic of smallpox had broken out in the Community at Saint-Laurent, and the infirmary in the "white house," the former novitiate, was filled with patients, both pupils and religious. A few died. Father Beaudet, the superior of the college, undertook the responsibility of nursing the quarantined patients. Brother André assisted the superior with pleasure, fearless of contagion though, because of his own weakness, he might easily have caught the disease. On his entry into the quarters of the sick he fell on his knees and prayed to Saint Joseph to remove the scourge. No further case of smallpox broke out and all the sick were restored to health. And yet but slight attention was paid to these facts. In everyone's opinion the porter continued to be the humble little Brother who was a bit eccentric.

Little by little, however, the pupils and their parents

[43]

became greatly attracted by the sweet simplicity and un-varying cordiality of the Brother who opened the door for them. During the long afternoons that the mothers spent in the parlors with their children, the less patient fathers came to smoke and to talk with the porter in his small room. The Brother, in conversations seasoned with much wit, profited by these opportunities to speak of his great devotion. People formed the habit of telling him about their troubles. He who had suffered so much himself understood them well and was easily moved to sympathy. While he gave them his own good counsel, he also reminded them of Saint Joseph, the consoler who is so powerful with the Heart of Jesus.

The genial doorkeeper welcomed every visitor with great amiability. One day, meeting a man with a sad and preoccupied appearance, he asked:

"How are things going at home?"

"What does that matter to you?" replied the stranger in an irritable and boorish manner.

The rebuff did not bother Brother André. As soon as the man had taken leave of his two children, the porter accosted him with a smile:

"You seem to be in a bad humor today."

The visitor, by way of apology, began to tell him about his troubles: "My wife is sick in bed, and has been so for many years."

"But she is not so sick as you think," the Brother answered simply; "in fact, she is anxious to see you come home and to hear about her children." Then, shaking hands with the amazed man, he added: "At this very moment she became better."

The visitor went away muttering: "What a queer prophet that porter is!"

He went home as fast as his horse could carry him. His wife, still pale from her long illness, was standing on the doorstep, smilingly waiting for him.

"How are the children?" she cried out gaily as he approached.

At the very moment when her husband had been talking to Brother André she had suddenly felt better and had insisted that her nurse should help her to rise. The latter had obeyed reluctantly. A few moments later, the woman had left her room to go to the balcony, where she anxiously awaited her husband's return.

More and more favors, spiritual as well as temporal, happened daily, and the report of them spread, so that visitors began to come especially to beg for the help of the saintly Brother. One of his confrères witnessed a strange scene:

"I am ready to certify by oath the truth of this incident: One Saturday late in November, 1884, I took the place of Brother André, who had to scrub the floor in the parlor. About five o'clock in the afternoon, somebody rang the doorbell. A lady, supported on the arms of two men, was ushered in. I asked what they wanted. One of the men replied:

" 'This lady wants to see Brother André.'

"The porter was at that moment on his knees scrubbing the entrance to the college.

" 'Brother André, this lady wishes to speak with you.'

"He paused in his work and asked, 'What can I do for you?'

" 'I am suffering from rheumatism. I want you to heal me.'

" 'Let her walk.'

"She began to walk a few steps, and the Brother kept on scrubbing the floor. After a moment, he said to the lady:

" 'You are no longer sick. You may go home.'

"She went out unassisted."

★

★   ★

Thus, twenty years previous to the beginning of Brother André's great work, he already gave evidence of God's predilection; but he gave no sign at that time that he was contemplating the erection of a shrine consecrated to Saint Joseph.

Opposite the college there was a small glade. Farther on, up the craggy mountain sides, the pale green of maples, oaks, and birches contrasted with the darker shades of the firs and pines. Here and there amid the groves extended patches of wasteland covered with brushwood. This site dominated the plain as far as the slightly elevated skyline of the blue Laurentians in the distance. From the mountain heights could be seen farms, groves, and villages with their steeples pointing heavenwards, and the meandering Rivière des Prairies with its banks bordered by trees. Lake Saint Louis in the westerly direction, fed by the Saint Lawrence River, gave the whole landscape a vivid appearance.

The religious, especially the novices, often ventured along the pathway far up the mountain. The owner of the land, a man of an irascible nature, denied everyone admittance to this picturesque spot and sometimes set his dogs on the intruders' heel. But for the novices, who, on taking the cassock, had not ceased to be fond of boyish pranks, this prohibition only added zest to the expedition. On holidays they generally slipped away to the top of Mount Royal. After a few moments of healthful recreation, they would recite the Office of the Blessed Virgin near a solitary birch tree which shaded a bare esplanade on the mountain-side.

The authorities of the college were desirous of possessing this piece of land, for they feared that some disorderly

resort might be built there. The purchase price was too
high, however. The property was meantime sold to a
French Canadian, who also asked too much for it. Then
an act of childlike faith succeeded when all human pro-
cedures had failed. Brother Aldéric, the bursar, who en-
tertained a most filial devotion to the Workman of Nazareth, especially since he had been cured through the intervention of Brother André, hid in the coveted ground a
medal of Saint Joseph. At least six years previously, the
little porter, driven by the desire of erecting a shrine here,
had, without saying a word about it, done the same thing.
In later life, he recommended this act of faith in Saint
Joseph as a means of evicting refractory proprietors. On
July 22, 1896, the purchase was made.

The devoted porter was the first to begin the work. He
immediately began to widen the footpath and to make
steps up the steep hills. Above the abrupt ascent of the
mountain spur was a glade of young shoots which the
workers christened "Saint Joseph's Boulevard." Father
Lafond, who was superintending the work, carved that
name in his fine handwriting on the steep side of a mountain bordering the spot.

The following year a small pavilion was built of rough-
hewn timber. A ladder gave access to the roof, which over-
looked across the trees the beautiful landscape. Brother
André had thus far said nothing about erecting a chapel in
honor of Saint Joseph, but he placed in a crevice of the
rock a small statue of his dear Saint and there in his spare
moments he used to pray. He also placed a small dish at
the foot of the statue, to receive the donations of casual
pilgrims. When the parlors were crowded with visitors,
he would talk about his projects with his friends, suggest-
ing to them that they climb up to "Saint Joseph's Boulevard" to see the magnificent view, and advising them
to say a little prayer near the statue in the rock.

How charming was this first shrine, so humble, so un-pretentious! Just a narrow path entangled with brushwood, a small statue, and an old dish wherein coins were to be deposited! What a touching scene of beauty was this rustic simplicity! And so it was with the pennies of the poor that Brother André was to build his first chapel, as well as the future crypt and the basilica, one of the finest temples in America.

Small donations came in gradually, and the porter, with the permission of his superiors, saved them for the place of pilgrimage of which he long had dreamed. From time to time he added to the sum the five cents he earned for cutting a student's hair. Poor as he was and indifferent to earthly possessions, he all his lifelong made no distinction between the smallest coins and very liberal offerings but received either with manifest joy. "It is all for Saint Joseph," he said as he counted the small coins.

The influence of the apostle of Saint Joseph on the people became more and more obvious. Every day brought its contingent of sick and afflicted, to each of whom he gave a hearty welcome and consoling words; and to all he spoke of Jesus and His Foster-Father. One day a young man came to him, leaning on the arm of another.

"Do you recognize me, Brother André?"

"You are my little companion who used to come and pray with me on the mountain. How are you?"

"Not at all well. About a month ago I had an accident while working. The doctor says I must go to the hospital. I have been told that my leg will have to be amputated, for it has become gangrened. You have the power to cure me if you wish, Brother André."

"No, not I, but Saint Joseph, if you have faith. Send back your carriage."

To protect the cripple from the gaze of the curious, Brother André escorted him into a room adjoining his small chamber. In the evening when no one could observe and criticize him, he brought the young man into his own room and rubbed the injured leg for a few moments. Swollen and black though it had grown, the limb became absolutely sound, so much so that the patient was able to walk home alone, though the roads were covered with icy, slippery snow.

Miracles became more and more numerous and were noised abroad in spite of the wonder-worker's recommendation to say nothing about them.

History, forever repeating itself, records an episode in the Bible: "The Lord said to Satan: Hast thou considered my servant Job, that there is none like him in the earth, a man simple, and upright, and fearing God, and avoiding evil, and still keeping his innocence?" (Job. II, 3). Then God permitted Satan to try his servant. It would seem that the evils of suffering inflicted on Job were repeated in the life of Brother André. Throughout his youth as a poor orphan without friends, he was tossed about from one house to another, and was constantly tortured with pain. In the religious life he was tried by rigid and stern superiors, while the condition of his health became steadily worse. Sometimes he who was permitted to heal others had to spend a few days in the infirmary, suffering from heartburn and racked by the convulsive spasms of chorea.

Now, another sharp distress tore his soul with anguish: everything seemed to unite to paralyze his influence. Some of the parents of the children attending the school protested because of the number of sick and afflicted persons who came to the college to seek help from Brother André. The authorities, yielding to these remonstrances, strictly forbade the porter to receive his suppliants during visiting hours and compelled him to meet them in a shabby little building on the other side of the street, opposite the college. They feared on the one hand to bring discredit upon their Community through being led astray by a religious who, though fervent, was illiterate and eccentric, and on the other hand to thwart the possible designs of Providence. Archbishop Bruchési of Montreal was in the same dilemma. He asked them:

"Would Brother André stop receiving the sick if you should tell him to do so?"

"He would obey blindly."

"Then let him alone. If his work is from God it will live; if not, it will crumble away."

Not all were animated by the same spirit of tolerance. A few confrères and especially the village doctor openly opposed the healer, flinging at him such nasty epithets as "fake-healer" and "quack-doctor."

Brother André continued the work without losing courage, though he often shed tears and poured forth his sorrow into the heart of a confrère who inspired him with confidence. He told him of his hopes, and expressed his grief at not having the help of a priest to hear the confessions of those who came to him. This companion witnessed many touching scenes during the few days he spent repairing the hovel in which Brother André would henceforth receive the clients of Saint Joseph.

Far from being satisfied with their partial victory, the disparagers went to the Archbishop's palace to state their grievances. A few confrères and the beneficiaries of Brother André's favors stood by the accused. The prelate, Archbishop Bruchési, with his usual prudence, dismissed both parties without letting them know his own sentiments.

Vexed at getting no support from the ecclesiastical authorities, the opponents then appealed to the civil authorities, claiming: "The board of health must absolutely take cognizance of this matter, for public health is at stake."

A delegate was sent by the board of health to bring this

contemner of medical laws to his senses. Brother André received him courteously and explained that his remedies —rubbing the afflicted with a medal or with a bit of oil— were by no means harmful. The delegate departed, greatly pleased at the Brother's common sense and urbanity.

To these trials were added calumnies attacking his reputation. Because he touched the sick in healing them, his enemies charged him with immodesty. This insult was even thrown into his face by a visitor to whom he had manifested much kindness and sympathy. Assaulted by these odious slanders, suspected in his own Community, violently attacked by outsiders, harassed in every way, he at last sought consolation in a layman who seemed to sympathize with him. In this man he placed the utmost confidence, trusting to him the secrets of his heart and sometimes shedding tears in his presence. This confidant, alas, was an ignoble person, incapable of loyalty and still more incapable of understanding the great, straightforward soul of his venerable friend, and he divulged the secrets intrusted to him. As he understood nothing of the action of the Holy Ghost in noble souls, he took Brother André for a fool. Joining the Brother's adversaries, he began to circulate the worst calumnies. Finally, his revolting treachery was made known. Brother André, who was very sensitive and of an exquisite delicacy and an absolute trustworthiness in matters of friendship, felt the wound keenly for a long time:

"My best friend, whom I trusted implicitly, has betrayed me. He has divulged everything I told him. You cannot imagine all the sorrow he has caused me."

The devil was indeed infuriated against a work which gave the promise of so much spiritual regeneration. These trials, however, but served to give more lustre to the patience, humility, meekness, obedience, and indomitable energy of the servant of God.

In the midst of the storm, a ray of light appeared in the darkened sky. Permission was given to erect the first shrine to Saint Joseph. At the end of the summer of 1904, Brother Abondius, the college carpenter, built on the promontory, half-way up the mountain, a small chapel, eighteen by fifteen feet. There were no windows: the sun's rays filtered through a double pane of ground glass extending along the arris of the roof. That miniature oratory, with a folding-door in front, looked like a lantern lost on the side of the mountain.

Brother André liked to recall an event which took place when the work began:

"A man came to see me at the college. He was so thin that one could almost see through him. He suffered from a cancer in the stomach and could scarcely eat. I said to him:

" 'Will you come and work for me tomorrow morning? We must widen the road to the chapel in the mountain.'

" 'I should be only too glad to do so, but I have not the strength to work. I cannot eat.'

" 'All right. Come anyhow and have breakfast with me tomorrow.'

"The following day I served him a good meal. The very same day he found himself able to work. All trace of his sickness had vanished. I kept him in my service for several months."

The nineteenth of November, 1904, was a day of exultation. The statue of Saint Joseph was blessed in the college chapel and was then carried in procession to the new sanctuary, where holy Mass was celebrated and the Stations of the Cross were erected. Let us pass over the numerous participants in this scene to contemplate, though perhaps the least in external rank, him whose story we are relating.

Brother André was approaching his sixtieth year. He appeared at this time as a shrewd, little old man, thin and hollow-eyed from illness and mental suffering, with curly hair turning gray, and yet with an air of irrepressible youth in his erect carriage, in his face and eyes, and especially in his smile. Wholly forgetful of his own struggles and troubles, he enjoyed the triumph of his loved friend, the Workman of Nazareth. This day it did not matter that his mission was far from being as yet fully approved and that his superiors merely tolerated his activity among the sick.

Scarcely was the chapel inaugurated when it had to be closed for the dreary winter months. By way of recompense, Brother André transformed into a shrine a nook adjoining the recreation hall. A few privileged ones came from time to time to pray before a statue of Saint Joseph placed in a niche. They also made the Way of the Cross in the chapel with the Brother porter, who made a silent meditation at each station and said a few prayers composed extemporaneously. This religious exercise was often performed in the evening, in the darkness. On one occasion a religious who knew nothing of the custom entered the chapel. A few pilgrims who had been concealed from his sight by the pews behind which they were kneeling, just then arose and proceeded to the next station. When the visitor saw these figures emerging from the obscurity he sprang up and shrieked, to the amusement of them all.

Brother André often gazed longingly across the barren trees at the Oratory on the mountain hooded with snow. Occasionally he went there, being greeted on the way by the children, who shouted and laughed as they slid down the snowclad slopes. The sick, being no longer permitted access to the college, sought meager shelter in the small building on the other side of the road, and waited till the porter could spare a few moments from his work to come to see them. With the return of spring, visitors began to arrive in crowds.

One afternoon there were about a hundred visitors scattered among the trees over the campus of the college. Brother André was raking the aisles between the flower-beds and apparently took no notice of them. At last a lady ventured to approach him, only to be told:

"Go and wait for me at the Oratory. I shall join you there when I am free."

During the holidays, when he could easily find a substitute porter, he spent entire days receiving visitors. Later on he confessed:

"Not infrequently I did not take the trouble of eating breakfast. I slipped a few biscuits into my pocket and went to the Oratory. Sometimes when I came back in the evening, I realized that I had forgotten to eat them."

As the years passed, the storm raged over his head more furiously than ever. Doctors and certain of the religious waged a desperate struggle against him. Up and down the city sceptics made fun of the "old fool" who pretended he could work miracles. Visitors to the college complained that the sick were blocking up the small station in front of the building. Wearied at all these remonstrances, the superiors thought of sending Brother André to another mission of their Congregation, the University of Saint Joseph in New Brunswick. Oftentimes the little Brother shed bitter tears, but he never lost courage. Rather, he declared: "What consoles me is to see that each great sorrow is followed by a new development at the Oratory."

One group of the religious defended Brother André warmly and went to Father Dion, the provincial, to ask him to enlarge the sanctuary, to heat it, and make it accessible in winter. This request was not considered opportune, however.

Proceedings at the diocesan center were not more su

cessful. This prudent reserve, quite legitimate on the part of authority, but served to show the divine character of Brother André's mission; and when at length Archbishop Bruchési and Father Dion were won over to the little apostle's side, they became his staunchest supporters.

Meantime, the people on all sides extolled the miracle-worker of Mount Royal. Numerous pilgrimages were organized, opposition crumbled away, and soon the work was openly triumphant. As yet the organization of it was only a half-opened flower, a bud which had suffered from the frost; soon, however, the rays of a beneficent sun were to bring it to its full bloom.

V

IN FULL BLOOM

WE SHALL give here only the main events in the prodigious development of the Oratory. Since it is not so much the history of the work as the life-story of its founder that interests us, we shall suppress all superfluous details, the better to bring into relief the personality of Brother André.

After the erection of the first chapel, the good religious continued for four years more to serve as porter of the College of Notre Dame. Whenever he had a free moment during the day he went to join the visitors who awaited him, and frequently in the evenings, holding a lantern in his hand, he took a few privileged ones to his little sanctuary to pray and make the Way of the Cross. Even at that early date pilgrimages were organized, though they were often forced to disband because of unforeseen storms. The chapel itself was kept closed all winter, even on the feast of Saint Joseph.

In 1906, a group of laymen, friends of Brother André, petitioned the superiori provincial to undertake the construction of a church n honor of Saint Joseph, but the project was deemed premature.

In July, 1908, a shelter, consisting merely of a roof supported by posts, was erected, thus extending the original shrine to the rocky mountain-side. Two months

later, half of this structure was walled up, to form the
nave of a church, of which the primitive chapel became
the sanctuary. From this time on, the Oratory was heated
during the winter and thus was made accessible to pilgrims
throughout the year.

In the spring of 1909 a pavilion was built. It included a
restaurant and rest-room for pilgrims, and a small cell and
an office for Brother André, who was henceforth relieved
of his work as porter at the college and was officially appointed guardian of the Oratory.

The following year, the nave was again enlarged and the
original chapel, now too small for the nave, was pro-
portionately lengthened at the other end. The ground floor
of this part was made into the sacristy. A small room for
Brother André was furnished under the roof. A steeple, in
which was hung a large bell, towered above the structure.

Though humble in proportions, the Oratory, situated
high on the mountain in a spot of great natural beauty,
presented a striking spectacle. On every side, nature in its
wild and rugged aspect charmed the eye of the beholder:
trees, stalwart and erect like giant sentinels keeping
guard; trees gnarled and bent; trees inviting to rest under
"their broad umbrageous branches"; rambling mazes of
undergrowth and thorn bushes; shrubs of brilliant hues;
wild wood-flowers and clinging vines creeping in exuberant
profusion from the crevices of the thickly carpeted slopes,
and, veiled in hazy purple beyond the fair expanse of plain
and suburbs, the distant mountains. The shrine was taking
on new life and rapid developments were exceeding all
anticipations.

At this time a presbytery was built, and again it was
necessary to enlarge the nave of the church, this time until
it extended to the shelter built against the mountain. In
November, 1912, Archbishop Bruchési of Montreal came
to bless this addition, and then addressed these words to

the crowd gathered within the edifice.

"Here I behold a pious enterprise which fills me with hope. This Oratory may justly be compared to the mustard-seed, which is the least of all and yet grows into a great tree. In the beginning, a simple and trusting hand placed a statue here; then daily prayers were offered before it; and soon a little chapel was built to house it. Then, as the clients of Saint Joseph became more and more numerous, his shrine had to be enlarged, again and yet again. It is the latest addition I have come to bless today. Yet the work is only in its infancy. I look into a future, a not too far distant future, to see a basilica worthy of Saint Joseph rising here on Mount Royal and facing the most magnificent of horizons."

The period of uncertainties, of hesitations, had at length come to an end. With blind confidence in Providence, the plan of an imposing granite basilica was conceived, one which would vie with the mountain itself in majesty.

In 1915, while the World War was destroying many of the churches of Europe, a vast stone crypt, resembling a huge bastion, was erected on Mount Royal. The bell-tower and the sanctuary of the first humble Oratory were brought there and were thus preserved, to form as it were the head and the neck of that body of stone made up of successive sections. The structure was set in a vast French landscaped garden, framed by closely planted poplar trees. The rough and irregular slopes were formed with much labor into beautiful terraces, thickly carpeted with grass.

In 1924, behind the crypt, which now served as a landing, the basilica began to rise from its bed, set deep in the rock. In the way of the medieval cathedrals, it rose by slow stages to majestic beauty. The work was interrupted for several years, and then was resumed in 1937, after Brother André made his magnificent gesture of faith:

"You wish to roof the basilica? You have only to place

a statue of Saint Joseph within the open walls, and he will soon provide a shelter for himself."

Topping Mount Royal, with high uplifted head, looms the dome of the basilica, its inspiration having been drawn from the celebrated dome of Florence designed by Brunelleschi. Owing to the possibilities of modern building materials, however, a contemporary master in architecture conceived a plan of much greater scope and daring. The interior of the sanctuary, when completed, will be a vast movement of harmoniously ascending lines, an incomparable symphony in warm-colored mosaics and stained-glass windows. From the small cupola at the summit of the dome, one can look out over the city below, swarming with its million and a half human beings.

To the east, far beyond the Saint Lawrence River, Mount Saint-Grégoire overshadows the birthplace of Brother André; to the west, on the immense plain extending as far as the sinuous smoky skyline of the Laurentians, are two more points fraught with memories: Notre Dame College and Saint-Laurent College, for in them lived the artisan who not only built the great sanctuary to the Patron of the Universal Church, but popularized devotion to him in America as well.

Numerical figures are dry but eloquent with truth when they testify as witnesses. These, then, bear witness to the importance of the work of the Oratory: More than ten million dollars have been spent on it. Every year, an average of two hundred thousand letters come to the Oratory from the four corners of the world to ask prayers and favors. Two hundred and fifty thousand copies of *The Annals of Saint Joseph*, a monthly review, are printed every issue. One confraternity includes more than thirty thousand members. Visitors to the shrine are numbered in the millions every year.

Though the splendor of the site may account in part

for the flow of tourists, it could not suffice as an explanation for the continual arrivals of thousands of pilgrims from all parts of America. Frequently, the lone pilgrim going up to the shrine to pray suddenly disappears in the midst of a newly arrived pilgrimage. From the heart of the city a whole parish sometimes winds its way through the noise and bustle of the streets towards Mount Royal.

Certain organizations, such as that of the Christian Laborers, bring in a human tide. On these occasions as many as fifty thousand visitors transform the terraces into a moving panorama of variegated colors. Upon the side of the mountain, a procession of singing and praying men, women, and children, winds its way between two lines of kneeling pilgrims, preceding the Blessed Sacrament escorted by the scarlet-robed acolytes and the priests in white and gold vestments.

At twilight, the great prayerful murmur of the long torch-bearing procession makes an unforgettable impression. Inspired by the collective fervor, the pilgrim is moved by but one desire: to be but a voice blended in prayer and song, an atom lost in that throng which God is drawing unto Himself. The Oratory is a place in which one comes palpably in contact with the supernatural, in which one breathes the very atmosphere of divine grace, in which human faith shows itself naked and unashamed. It is an oasis to which we all, poor way-worn travellers to eternity, may come for spiritual regeneration, for strength to take up anew the battles of life. Here, temporal favors are the allurements Christ makes use of as He did in the days of His earthly life to draw the hearts of men. Along the St. Lawrence River one may often see fish swept in on the tide from the deep waters and caught in traps when the tide recedes. So is the shrine of Saint Joseph a divine fishing net into which the incoming tide of visitors sweeps sinners and then, when it recedes, leaves them imprisoned

[61]

within the Master's love.

Concerning the divine work of the Oratory Archbishop Gauthier made a clear pronouncement in his Circular Letter of April 14, 1937. After recalling the exhortation of the Holy Father to have recourse to Saint Joseph in the great war of the Catholic Church against atheistic Communism, the spiritual leader of the diocese added:

"There has long been practiced in Montreal this confident recourse to Saint Joseph, and it has been marked by an extraordinary intensity since the foundation of the Oratory on Mount Royal. I can say of what has happened here only what all the world knows. It is palpably visible in the atmosphere of the great pilgrimages. No one comes here without leaving a better person. I can never think without deep emotion of the bounteous mercy here poured out. All the cares, all the sorrows of our great city come to beat as a wave against the promontory on which Saint Joseph has his domicile. There the great Saint welcomes us, always tender, always pitiful towards our miseries. How honored and filled with confidence we should be because Saint Joseph extends his powerful arms above our city to bless and protect it."

Such a prodigious growth cannot be ascribed to human means; only the special action of Providence can account for it. The first chapel, the crypt, and the basilica, were built by the millions of coins offered by those who received favors at Mount Royal. The amount given by the merely curious, by the tourists, is far less than one would suppose. Donations of considerable sums are almost unknown. The Lord prefers the alms inspired by a supernatural motive, the offerings of the poor, given as a token of gratitude.

That the development of this work is replete with the marvellous can be revealed by a few examples. A young professor, Father Adolphe Clément, being threatened with the loss of his sight, had to resign his professorship and was then appointed chaplain for the first Oratory. One evening when he was walking with Brother André, he expressed his desire:

"If you want me to work for Saint Joseph, you must get me back my sight. I can no longer read my Breviary, and it is only with the greatest difficulty that I can read the Mass."

"Tomorrow, you can begin the recitation of your Breviary," the Brother answered simply.

For twenty-five years this priest devoted himself to his duties at the Oratory, much to the astonishment of oculists, who sometimes said to him:

"We cannot understand how, with eyes like yours, you are able to read."

The story of another associate of Brother André deserves mention here, for it reads like one of those enchanting legends to be found in some illuminated manuscript of the great ages of faith. A sexagenarian was living alone on a patch of ground which he had cleared in a lifelong struggle against the forest. His wife had just died, and his son, the only survivor of his numerous children, had gone to seek his fortune far from home. The old man, Joseph Malenfant, had nothing to do except live peacefully and independently on his little estate at Saint-Hubert de Témiscouata, some three hundred miles east of Montreal. His peace was disturbed, however, by a strange and obsessing dream in which he saw an old man trying painfully to build a church and heard him calling to him for help. At length he concluded:

"This dream seems to be inspired by Heaven. To remove all my doubts in the matter I shall go in search of the old man who is asking my assistance."

When his friends and acquaintances ridiculed the import of his dream, he replied with his favorite maxim, which indicates his self-sacrificing devotedness:

"Not to help others is to be useless. It is better to obey God than man."

He at once set out for Montreal. There he heard of the sanctuary on the mountain. As he was climbing up the path to the Oratory, he came upon the old man he had seen in his vision. Brother André himself related the incident:

"As I was going down the mountain, I saw a man looking at me. I crossed the road and said to him: 'You are just the man I need.' "

After this, Mr. Malenfant begged of the authorities to admit him into the Community as a lay-Brother, but he was refused because of his advanced age. Not disheartened and still desirous to serve, he conceived a bold scheme for helping Brother André. He resolved to travel over the whole province from east to west, asking alms for the Oratory of Saint Joseph. With this end in view, he made his way to Chicoutimi, and asked authorization to beg alms in that diocese. Having no credentials to show that he was sent on a special mission, he was refused the privilege. Still untroubled in heart, he began his life as a vagabond of Saint Joseph, repeating from village to village, his slogan:

"Not to help others is to be useless. It is better to obey God than man."

To the refusals, insults, and difficulties he met with, temptations to discouragement now were joined. Later he confided:

"Often Satan whispered in my ear: 'You are an old fool, Malenfant. You had a fine farm, an assured livelihood, and now look at yourself: you are a tramp, a beggar, a good-for-nothing; you sleep in barns, you tramp the highways.' But I answered him: 'Begone, Satan! Not to help others is to be useless.' "

After traversing the province, he came back to the

Oratory and gave Father Dion the round sum of fourteen hundred dollars. The latter accepted the gift but asked Mr. Malenfant not to continue his vagabond life. Unaccustomed to the dignified and reserved demeanor of this priest, the old man said to one of the religious:

"Your superior is not a man; he is an icicle."

Soon, however, driven by his motto: "To assist no one is to be of no use," Mr. Malenfant was again wending his way on his mission. On the advice of a priest, he began to solicit subscriptions for *The Annals of Saint Joseph*. Of this he said:

"I have decided to 'analyze' the whole country."

For ten years until his death in July, 1924, he continued his wandering life. In the summer time he went sometimes to New Brunswick and even to Labrador, and he was lodged at the Shrine for several winters. He alone procured about thirty-five thousand subscriptions to the magazine.

★
★   ★

Passing over the numerous collaborators associated with the work accomplished on Mount Royal, let us lay stress on the work of the humble lay-Brother who still presided over the extending of the devotion to Saint Joseph. A multitude of charming incidents could be gleaned from this period of his life. He tells us:

"For a long time it was my duty to clean the Oratory. I was also sexton and I often served five or six Masses, one after another. One morning, when a strange priest arrived, there was not a single altar bread remaining. I ran so fast to the college to get a host that I got back without making him wait."

Vigilant, active, indefatigable, he kept everything in and around the church perfectly neat and clean. One year, a few days before Christmas, he pointed out to the bursar that the pavement in the crypt needed scrubbing. The latter forgot all about it. So, one evening, Brother André, with the help of a lay-Brother from Notre Dame College, set about the scrubbing. Had not the Father Provincial fortunately surprised him in the act and sent him to bed, he would have spent the whole night at the work.

Meantime, the little old man who was so humble and who made himself the servant of his confrères was fast becoming in the public mind the living image of Saint Joseph. As the pilgrims said:

"We come to pray to Brother André's Saint Joseph; we come to see Brother André."

Here, as at Lourdes, a florescence of favors manifested the action of God. For the miraculous spring of Lourdes was substituted the touch or the word of the humble Brother.

In 1912 the Archbishop of Montreal, when showing the crowd the votive offerings left at the Oratory, proclaimed:

"Shall I say that miracles are wrought here? Were I to deny the facts, these ex-votos, witnesses of all species of suffering, would contradict me."

Almost every favor was obtained by the mediation of Brother André, who during the day gave audience to the pilgrims, and spent a part of the night in prayer. We can select, here and there, a few typical cases related by the witnesses themselves. These are facts that could not be invented, and they alone can suggest the atmosphere at the Oratory.

One day, overwhelmed by the number of the visitors and unable to receive them one by one, Brother André went into the waiting room, took his stand behind the counter containing religious souvenirs, and asked each visitor in succession what he wanted. To each one he gave substantially the same answer:

"Rub yourself with the medal and with Saint Joseph's oil. Make a novena."

Then his gaze was riveted for a moment on one cripple: "Give me your crutches. Now, walk."

The cripple complied, and was so overjoyed at finding himself cured that he could not utter one syllable. Overcome with emotion, he turned, dashed out, ran down the hill, and got on the first street car that passed by. Those who saw the miracle stood gaping with astonishment. Without any interruption, Brother André continued:

"And what can I do for you, sir?"

"My arm is paralyzed; I cannot move it."

"Go to confession and then start a novena."

"I beg your pardon."

"I said: 'Go to confession and then start a novena.'"

"But I haven't gone to confession for the last twenty-five years."

Vainly the young lady who accompanied the stranger pulled at his arm, saying:

"Be careful, father, people will hear what you say."

"If I have been bad enough to spend twenty-five years without going to confession, I should be brave enough to admit it."

Brother André interrupted him: "Take your hat with your right hand and put it on."

The man obeyed, not a little stupefied at the surprise of feeling no more pain. Brother André continued:

"Come tonight to sleep in the room under the chapel roof. Tomorrow you will receive Holy Communion."

The recipient of the miracle went away. One of the bystanders said to Brother André:

"You have let him go. Do you think he will come back?"

"Yes, I am sure of it."

The man did come back, went to confession, and

received Holy Communion. Brother André delighted in describing the exuberant joy of this convert.

On another occasion, a few moments before the service usually held at the Oratory at three o'clock in the afternoon, Brother André left his office to attend the devotions. On his way he was accosted by a friend:

"Brother André, I have something important to ask of you."

"Come after the service."

"Perhaps that will be too late, for my sister-in-law is dying. I have been asked to recommend her to you."

"She is in good health."

"You misunderstood me. She is at the point of death."

Without making answer, Brother André went on his way to the crypt. The following day, the petitioner received a telephone call:

"Guess who is speaking."

"I recognize your voice—but no, that is impossible. I must be mistaken. The person I thought you are was anointed and is probably dead at this moment."

"No, it is really I, your sister-in-law. Yesterday afternoon, between two-forty-five and three o'clock, I was suddenly cured. I came to the city last night and I am now on my way to the Oratory."

Shortly afterwards, the same man accompanied to Brother André's office a woman with a stiff arm, the after-effect of a long illness.

"Brother André, please rub her arm."

"No, take your medal of Saint Joseph and rub her yourself."

As a matter of fact, Brother André always showed himself scrupulously reserved on this point. In vain had his enemies sent to him women who insisted on being taken care of by him so they might have a pretext to slander him. In this case, the man declared:

"As I applied the medal to her stiff wrist, I kept looking at Brother André, who was praying in front of me. At the precise moment that he closed his eyes, I felt her arm become perfectly flexible."

At times, merely the sight of the Brother was sufficient to work a cure. For example, a man wasted with tuberculosis and doomed to swift death was taken to the Oratory. Lost in the closely packed ranks of petitioners, he caught only a glimpse of the little religious and forthwith said to his wife, who was with him:

"I need not wait my turn, for I feel perfectly cured. Let us go to the church to thank God and give the offering promised in return for my restoration to health."

The very next day he returned to his work and never felt any recurrence of the disease.

There were many eyewitnesses of the following signal wonder. A great contingent of American visitors had thronged round the doors of the office all morning. At dinner-time, the Brother returned to the rectory. He was already mounting its steps under the eyes of hundreds of pilgrims, when a man went up the steps to stop him and to show him, through the open door of an ambulance that had forced its way amid the tumultuous crowd, a man lying on a stretcher.

"Untie him and let him walk," said the Brother simply, and went on into the house without further ado. The sick man got up and walked barefooted through the madly enthusiastic crowd.

Such facts, recorded by the hundreds, explain the presence of the throngs of pilgrims. Brother André, however, sought the healing of souls far more than the healing of bodies, and this healing was always his primary care. Even when dense crowds besieged his office, he would willingly spend over an hour working for the conversion of a sinner, though the reception of a sick man was generally the matter of a moment. He repeatedly explained that temporal favors are but means conducive to spiritual regeneration.

The Lord draws man to Himself by that natural instinct which leads him to pray for temporal favors. Anxious to win souls, He makes use of the word or the touch of His servant, of a relic, of a drop of oil, as means to effect His favors, just as during His earthy life, He used a little clay in order to heal the man who had been blind from birth.

Brother André constantly directed towards Saint Joseph the marvellous attraction he himself exerted on the crowds. With winning charm he conjured up the figure of the Nazarene Carpenter, contrasting his life of submission, of obedience, and of trials with the spirit of pride and sensuality that is so prevalent nowadays even among Christians. One of his constant companions said that he used to talk about Saint Joseph and the Holy Family with the ease and simplicity of one who is talking about well-known ancestors, and that he prayed to Saint Joseph just as if he were conversing with him.

His devotion to the holy Patriarch was instrumental in directing the affection of the faithful towards Jesus suffering. At night, when he was returning from visiting the sick, he always made the Way of the Cross with the companion who drove him back. Of this experience one of his friends said:

"When I made the Way of the Cross with him and heard him composing extemporaneously long and touching prayers, he seemed like one of the Apostles, those ignorant fishermen who yet were inexhaustible on the subject of Christ. It generally took about an hour; it seemed that he could not stop, so absorbed was he in God. His prayer usually resembled a conversation with an invisible interlocutor. He would stop to listen to the answer and then continue to talk."

Gradually a circle of his friends began to take part in this religious exercise, and thus originated the public Way of the Cross, which has been made every Friday at the Oratory for the last thirty years.

The Holy Hour, which takes place on the same evening, began in a similar manner. Brother André used to invite a few companions to the chapel. Then, in the darkness, he would light a candle and set it on his prie-dieu and would then continue his prayer until the candle was completely burnt. These services became so well attended that he requested the Father Rector to preside over them.

Such is, in brief, the work accomplished on Mount Royal by an obscure little lay-Brother of Holy Cross. Its prodigious flowering was effected by the power of his profound faith and of his blind fidelity to divine inspirations. Indeed, he sometimes declared:

"Saint Joseph told me to place the Oratory in that spot."

This assertion seems to imply, not so much a genuine apparition as an interior voice. This opinion is confirmed by a letter from Archbishop Bruchési:

"Concerning Brother André, I should like to relate an interesting fact which, so far as I am aware, is not generally known. When Father Dion came with Brother André to see me about erecting the Oratory on Mount Royal, I called attention to the greatness and the expense of the undertaking and asked the good Brother if he were not afraid to begin it. He answered in the negative. Then I said to him:

" 'Brother, I have something to ask you. Is there anything of a supernatural character in what you are doing? Do you think you have visions? Did good Saint Joseph make you understand that he wants a temple on Mount

Royal?'

"To this he answered: 'There is nothing of that kind. I have only my great devotion to Saint Joseph. This it is that guides me and gives me full confidence.'

"Such frankness, such humble and beautiful simplicity struck me forcibly."

Just as the pilgrim, after contemplating from a distance the Oratory on the side of the mountain, approaches nearer and nearer, and then enters the sombre crypt where he seeks the altar and kneels close to it to pray, so let us, now that we have looked at the exterior life and work of Brother André, try to penetrate into his inner self, coming step by step into that sanctuary till we enter with deep respect into the veiled splendor of his intimate union with God.

VI

CONFIDENCE

IN CONFORMITY with our plan of relating the life of Brother André in the simplest manner possible, let us come with no preconceived ideas to the study of his soul, applying the method of the photographer rather than that of the painter, so as sketch reality; that is, the characteristic features of his personal sanctity. Let us not try to describe his virtues by a set order of their dignity; rather, let us note them as they flower forth in his daily living among us. Let us describe in the order in which they come to our habitual notice three dominant traits of his character: an unchangeable faith, an unfailing humility, a heroic charity.

When Brother André's friends and fellow religious were asked for their impression of his holiness, they followed this same order in their reply. One of them declared: "He was a man of extraordinary faith." He then cited a few instances to prove the point, and concluded: "In spite of that, he showed not the slightest trace of pride."

We shall elaborate somewhat on the self-sacrifice and the devotions of this servant of God; and we shall complete our sketch taken from real life by pointing out a few points of resemblance, physical and moral, between Brother André and the Curé of Ars.

There was no end to the confidence of Saint Joseph's

apostle, with the result that his whole existence was woven with divine marvels. Never did he yield to the least discouragement during the delays before the realization of the extraordinary work entrusted to him by Divine Providence. During his whole life his prayers were offered, not to beg favors, but to thank God in advance for the liberality on which he set his hope. Endeavoring to retain the savour that characterizes the narrative of the eye-witness, we shall now recall certain incidents which demonstrate the unwavering faith of Brother André.

On one occasion an unfortunate victim of an accident was carried to the Oratory. His gangrened legs were like meat boiled to shreds, and the doctor had declared they must be amputated immediately, telling the patient, who still cherished the hope of being cured without this cruel remedy:

"It is as impossible to save you without this surgery as it would be to cause the St. Lawrence River to flow up-stream."

A witness who saw Brother André, despite this verdict, delicately rub the mutilated flesh of the poor man, said:

"Surely Saint Joseph is not going to make new legs grow. There is nothing left."

Undisturbed, the humble Brother continued to attend to his patient till he was made well.

Once Brother André was called to the bedside of a dying mother, only to be told on his arrival:

"Alas, you are too late!"

The doctor, judging that she could live only a few moments, had already given the death certificate. Her relatives, believing her dead, had covered her face with a veil.

Brother André knelt by the bed, unveiled the face of the supposed dead woman, and touched her lightly. She opened her eyes. Then, becoming fully reanimated, she murmured:

"I am hungry."

The good old man gave her a piece of orange to eat. One can only recall the scene in the Gospel in which our dear Lord said to Jairus, after raising his daughter to life: "Give her something to eat."

Another mother brought to Brother André her young son, whose weakened spine could not hold his body erect. In this case the Brother simply declared him cured. The overjoyed mother at once took off the plaster cast and iron rod that held her son's body and head in position. The superior vainly tried to dissuade her from such imprudence; but the little boy, on being freed from his harness, began immediately to romp about.

A certain man was so afflicted with rheumatism that he could not suffer even the lightest touch without loud groans of anguish. Brother André vigorously rubbed the afflicted limbs, then asked: "Do you feel better?" Again rubbing them, he said:

"Stand up now; you are cured."

A woman with cancer went to the Oratory and Brother André declared her cured. Her doctor, who had decided to operate on her, refused to believe in the miracle and began the operation, only to find no trace of the cancer.

The following occurrence was related by Brother André to show the goodness of Saint Joseph and to remind us that those miraculously cured do not need the help of the surgeon's knife. An operation had been pronounced necessary for a woman with a very large tumor in her back. Before undergoing it, she came to the Oratory, where all trace of her trouble disappeared. On the day appointed for the operation, she came to the hospital and asked to be examined once more. The doctor, to his great amazement, could discover no trace of the growth and finally asked in a bewildered way:

"On which side was the tumor?"

When a certain patient recommended himself to the prayers of Brother André before undergoing an operation, he was told:

"Do not have an operation; pray to Saint Joseph instead."

The friends who often accompanied the revered Brother on his visits to the sick testify that no one had to regret the following of such advice. Such an absolute confidence in Divine Providence, far from being temerity, indicates rather a constant submission to the inspirations of God.

"How dare you make such decisions without hesitation?" asked a priest. "If I were you, I should be afraid of tempting the Lord."

"It is easy to see that Saint Joseph is going to heal them," replied the Brother.

"Why do you content yourself with urging some persons to pray, while to the others you say bluntly: 'Give up your crutches; if you cannot walk, it is because you are lazy'? Why this difference?"

The old man paused for a moment and then said: "Oftentimes, you see, it is obvious that they are cured."

From these answers we see that Saint Joseph was his inspiration and guide during the long hours he devoted to the alleviation of human miseries.

Brother André demanded this same confidence from those who sought his aid. When someone complained because his prayer was only half heard, he said:

"If you do not wish to lose what you have obtained, continue to pray."

To an importunate person who cried: "Cure me, cure me!" he replied: "You will not be cured because you lack confidence in God. You come to demand that I cure you, as if I were a doctor. If God owes you anything, go ask it of Him."

Here is another narrative from an intimate friend of Brother André: "I was talking with the Brother when a crippled young man came in. He declared:

" 'I have waited long enough. My novena ends tomorrow, and if I am not cured, I will have my leg amputated.'

"Brother André replied: 'As you like. Do you want me to call up the surgeon right now?'

"The young man went out, exasperated. I hurried to follow him.

" 'That is a fine way to receive people,' he said to me. 'I will never return here.' "

" 'You are only punishing yourself,' I answered. 'How long has your doctor been attending you?' "

" 'Five years.' "

" 'Did he do you any good? Yet, far from getting angry at him, you have paid him for his services. And now, because Brother André, who receives you out of pure kindness, does not heal you, you are furious. Listen to me, my friend, go back to see him and do whatever he tells you.' "

The young man complied, and Brother André was so certain his confidence and submission would be rewarded that he simply said to him: "Begin another novena in honor of Saint Joseph. If, on the ninth day, you are not cured, I myself will amputate your leg."

A woman completely paralyzed in both legs was carried to the Oratory. An assistant to Brother André, who received the pilgrims and kept them in line, asked them kindly to let the woman be taken to the Brother immediately, adding that there might be a miracle. The paralytic with the four persons accompanying her came into the office. Suddenly, through the thin partition came the raised voice of the Brother. All listened attentively.

"Get up and walk."

"Oh, no, I cannot. My legs are completely paralyzed."

"Woman of little faith, I command you: get up and walk."

Suddenly, in the doorway, the miraculously cured woman appeared, tears streaming from her eyes, dumb with overwhelming emotion. Amid the wild enthusiasm of the witnesses, she walked, strong and erect.

At times Brother André demanded of his clients a blind, heroic faith. A farmer who had been injured by a mowing-machine went to the Shrine. He was told:

"Take your crutches into the church. Tomorrow you shall resume your work."

The man obeyed, limping painfully.

"Don't you see that you are not cured?" said his companions.

The injured man, not at all dismayed, followed the order given and went back to work the next day. With much effort he managed to plough, or rather, to crawl along behind his plough. When evening came, in spite of sarcastic remarks and the pain of his swollen feet, he still remained hopeful. The next morning he awoke perfectly cured.

Another man came to Brother André's office to tell him: "My sister is afflicted with a cancer in her chest which has caused caries in three of her ribs. An emergency operation is, according to the doctor, the only means of saving her."

"Tell her not to be operated on, that Saint Joseph will heal her."

Every day at noon, the petitioner came back to say: "My sister is getting worse; she is going to die."

And he was reassured, "If she has no other disease, she will not die."

In return for her heroic confidence the patient, at the

moment when even surgery was declared of no avail, was completely cured, the cancer disappeared, and the ribs that had been thoroughly destroyed, were made perfect again.

This was the confidence that Jesus exacted from those for whom He worked miracles: sometimes before manifesting His power, He would ask the sick whether they believed that He was indeed the Son of God and had power to heal them.

A miracle is never a vainglorious display of power. Our Saviour withdrew when the Jews, to satisfy their curiosity, asked Him to work wonders. Likewise are the favors bestowed at the Oratory not intended to gratify idle curiosity.

One person went on eight successive days to Brother André's office in the hope of seeing some striking wonder, and was finally told: "Because you lack faith in the power of God and are animated only by vain curiosity, you shall not see a miracle." At length she decided to remain at home. The very next day a paralytic was instantaneously cured.

The recommendations made by Brother André to his petitioners were an excellent means to exact blind confidence: "Rub yourself with a medal; use a little of Saint Joseph's oil; deprive yourself of some particular food."

Many who did not fear the most rigorous penances, or long pilgrimages on foot, or the most painful medical treatments, despised such simple methods. Before granting favors, God exacts blind confidence. To rub oneself with a medal seems indeed very puerile; but it is not puerile, in order to comply with such an injunction, to renounce one's own judgment and surrender oneself to God. Only those who put these counsels faithfully into practice obtained their cure, not because of any intrinsic efficacy in the means suggested, but because of the supernatural confidence required to use such means.

Brother André often said: "Many of the sick are not cured because of their lack of faith and conformity to the will of God. They will not do what I ask of them; indeed, one must have faith to rub oneself with a medal or with oil. . . . We must pray to Saint Joseph, but always and in everything will nothing but what God wills."

For the same reason he recommended: "Always hold a medal of Saint Joseph in your hand when making a request, having an interview, or transacting an important affair. Holding a medal in one's hand makes one think more of Saint Joseph than wearing it. Such a practice is a proof of great confidence."

He advanced no other reason when he suggested burying a medal in a coveted property, or depositing one in a house which the owner obstinately refused to sell.

One may well ask whether Brother André believed in any inherent power in the means proposed. Usually he demanded the privation of chocolate, cake, or cigarettes merely as a measure of mortification, which would, he may have considered, be a remedy for some very mild disorders for which he thought it useless to disturb Saint Joseph.

His extraordinary power of curing by mere touch was amazing. He sometimes told his intimate friends about the great wonders that God accomplished by means of "trifling instruments." For example:

"A man who had been wounded while hunting came to see me in my office. The lead pellet remaining in the flesh had caused poisoning, and the doctors had decided to cut off his hand. I rubbed him, and the infected flesh trickled down to the floor like melted grease. My hands were all greasy from it. He went away perfectly cured."

He was asked why he rubbed the sick, and made answer: "My hands produce the same effect as Saint Joseph's oil."

Those blinded by preconceived theories will scoff at anything so "childish." Most certainly, rubbing a limb affected with cancer and obtaining an almost instantaneous cure is a means much out of proportion to the result obtained. But there was divine intervention lurking in these actions. Christ Himself acted in the same manner, as we see in the cases of the deaf and dumb man and the man born blind. The Gospel tells us:

"And they bring to Him one deaf and dumb; and they besought Him that He would lay His hand upon him. And taking him from the multitude apart, He put His fingers into his ears, and spitting, He touched his tongue; and looking up to heaven, He groaned, and said to him: Ephpheta, which is, Be thou opened. And immediately his ears were opened, and the string of his tongue was loosed, and he spoke right. . . .

"And they bring to Him a blind man, and they besought Him that He would touch him. And taking the blind man by the hand, He led him out of the town; and spitting upon his eyes, laying His hands on him, he asked him if he saw anything. And looking up, he said: I see men as it were trees, walking. After that again He laid His hands upon his eyes, and he began to see, and was restored, so that he saw all things clearly."

It would have been easy for Our Saviour to work miracles by a single word; but He had recourse to simple means with a view to awakening faith in the hearts of those who sought His aid. The same motive prompted Brother André to act likewise. Thus he was able to repeat to the pilgrims whose prayers were heard the word of the Master: "Thy faith hath made thee whole; go thy way in peace."

Although cures were usually worked by the contact of

Brother André's hands, sometimes they were granted through a mere word. For example, on one occasion at a gathering at the home of one of his friends, he spoke for an hour on the Passion of our dear Lord. A lady who had suffered for many years from ankylosis of the knee wanted to see him in the hope of being cured.

"I have been told that you are crippled; but I do not believe it, for you are not sick. Kneel, try, do," he said to her smiling.

The woman knelt without the least discomfort.

Another case in which God's intervention at Brother André's request was apparent concerns an assistant doctor at the Hôtel-Dieu Hospital, Montreal, who was so afflicted with phlebitis that he could no longer use one of his legs and would, according to expert opinion, have to use crutches for the rest of his life. On the advice of a friend, he had recourse to Brother André, who said to him: "You are a physician; have confidence: Saint Joseph will not permit such a fine career to be ruined and all the sacrifices made by your parents to be wasted. Leave your crutches there and walk to the door."

The cripple walked the distance back and forth, and then Brother André said to him: "Now, take your crutches to the Shrine and thank Saint Joseph for so great a favor."

One day eight doctors at a meeting in the home of one of their friends were disparaging Brother André's cures, to this effect:

"Your Brother André is an impostor who does not know even the elements of medicine and who prescribes oil and medals for the sick. You cannot cite one genuine miracle performed by him."

The only rebuttal offered by the one challenged was the recital of the cure of the young physician. The others continued, however, to scoff and to challenge him anew. So he sent for the one who was cured. As this young doctor lived in the neighborhood, he was soon on the spot. Upon his arrival he was greeted with the question:

"Is it true that Brother André told you to leave aside your crutches and walk?"

"Of course it is true, and furthermore, I do not now feel the slightest pain."

★
★   ★

One may well wonder why all these favors were granted in the name of Saint Joseph. Doubtless they were given for the purpose of strengthening in the hearts of the people two virtues which are becoming almost extinct: confidence and faith. Of the number and frequency of these favors one of the Brother's faithful friends declared:

"For more than fifteen years, I came almost every afternoon to Brother André's office. I believe that not a single week passed without my witnessing some miracle. Now a paralytic was cured, now a blind man received his sight. Sometimes Brother André said to me: 'It cannot be asserted that these are always miracles, but they are great favors bestowed by God that people may open their eyes. Despite them, however, they seem to remain blind.' "

Though Brother André undeniably fostered faith in the hearts of the people, he did not succeed to the full extent of his ardent desires. The Lord leaves everyone free to believe; He forces no one. In the face of the most striking miracles, a soul can still resist grace; the Jews wanted to kill Jesus and His friend Lazarus whom He had raised from the dead, lest the people should believe in Him.

This first great lesson taught by Brother André's life recalls to mind a scene at the Oratory which was secretly filmed during its occurrence. A dense crowd waited at the door. Brother André, serious, thoughtful, and weary, slowly advanced. As he crossed the threshold, a woman stole up behind him and knelt to touch the hem of his cassock. Her gesture of confidence, of simple faith, recalls the the Gospel narrative:

"And behold a woman who was troubled with an issue of blood twelve years, came behind Him and touched the hem of His garment. For she said within herself: If I shall touch only His garment, I shall be healed."

It is best to leave to those authorized the task of dealing with these miracles in detail, of giving names, circumstances, and testimonials from doctors. As the long train of afflicted, of cripples, of paralytics, of cancerous patients passes before our eyes, it would be most interesting to classify these many cures and compare them with analogous facts recorded in the Gospel. Could one but use the exquisite style of the *Fioretti* in depicting the scenes amid which Saint Francis of Assisi and his followers lived, great would be the charm of these modern narratives of how Brother André healed a man ill in body and in soul, of how Brother André detected the secrets of conscience, of how Brother André learned about a person's death at a time when no one could possibly have any knowledge of it. There is found in Brother André's life and works the same childlike faith, the same lively sense of the supernatural, the same literalness in the following of Christ as is found in the life and works of the great mystic of the thirteenth century.

Miracles, or at least extraordinary favors, were numbered in the thousands. "How good God is!" said Brother André again and again. Almost all those who visited the Shrine could tell of some miracle witnessed by them. So bewildering is the truth that it is well nigh unbelievable, and it is simply impossible to give a detailed account of everything that happened. We have culled only a few of Brother André's "little flowers" in order to show God's wonderful dealings with him and the sweet perfume of response drawn from the soul of the "Miracle Man."

His conduct was so balanced and his care to avoid the least bit of charlatanism was so painstaking that those who pretended to have received from him skill to cure the sick have been proved to be impostors or victims of hallucination. Their presumption would seem incredible had not writings from these so-called wonder-workers been handed over to us by the religious authorities.

Not all we find in Brother André is imitable. Nothing could be better than to try to imitate his virtues; but no one, unless invested by God Himself with a mission of this kind, can dare to arrogate to himself the privilege of saying to a sick person who, naturally speaking, can be saved only by an urgent operation: "Do not undergo surgery; you are cured." The afflicted person may, of course, by reason of his confidence in God or the saints, make such a decision; but no one, unless impelled unmistakably by divine inspiration, can assume the responsibility of giving such advice.

Brother André always asserted positively that he was not the possessor of any occult power. When asked by what magic he worked cures, he became very indignant and turned away those who dared to utter such an insult to his miraculous work, which he ascribed solely to the agency of God. An incident showed how much he was in earnest on this score. A stranger remarked to him: "You are better than Saint Joseph! We obtain from you all kinds of favors, but Saint Joseph turns a deaf ear to our petitions."

So indignant was the frail old man at this want of understanding that he became ill. Seized with a convulsive tremor, he had to be brought to his room. He said of the experience: "I began to tremble, and I had to stay in bed several days, for I was unable to control my nervous agitation."

[85]

The secret of Brother André must, then, be found only in his unwavering faith in Providence. God alone was the immediate agent of the numerous miracles that took place at the Shrine as a means to establish devotion to Saint Joseph.

VII

HUMILITY

IN THE Magnificat, the Blessed Virgin gives us an example of true humility. Thus does she praise the Lord: "My soul doth magnify the Lord. He that is mighty hath done great things to me; and holy is His name." Though we know that true humility is truth, few of us have a real concept of this virtue. We persuade ourselves that to practice humility we must shrivel up within ourselves and proclaim that we are nothing, that we can do nothing, that we dare not, for fear of pride, speak of God or do works of zeal. The true saint is indeed filled with self-contempt because he sees himself mirrored in the radiance of the divine Light, and yet the knowledge of his human limitations does not keep him from undertaking great things, for he knows that his weakness is made strong by the power of the Most High. True humility consists, not in disavowing the talents God has given us, but in acknowledging Him as their Author.

This principle of truth formed the basis of Brother André's whole life. Though he knew that in so far as natural talents were concerned, he was the least gifted member of his Community, yet, once convinced of God's designs, he pleaded neither ignorance nor weakness as an excuse to evade the divine behest. Hence, he undertook and accomplished a work that the saintly and scholarly

Bishop Bourget of Montreal, despite his ardent desire, had failed to effect in the forty years of his episcopate. Brother André kept on courageously with his work as if unaware of the opposition encountered in the first steps of his enterprise. Undaunted courage in surmounting the thousand and one obstacles that arose on every side was his only response to the taunts of those who taxed him with madness. He never faltered but, rather, went steadily forward with the unwavering assurance of a conqueror. Docile to the voice of God, he was fashioned of the same fibre as Joan of Arc, who replied to those who called her a visionary, "I will go on even if, in the attempt, I should wear my limbs to the knees."

Brother André was firmly convinced that God does not need human abilities, but glories in working with weak instruments. He knew well that the parable of the talents applies to the supernatural, and that God crowns in Heaven the fruits of His own gifts.

Though the apostle of Saint Joseph was well aware of his ignorance, he was none the less conscious of the marvels God was accomplishing through him. His own words spoken in connection with the following incident prove this. One afternoon, towards the end of the summer of 1936, two persons were cured. One was a sick woman who, carried in the arms of a friend, began to walk without difficulty; the other was a paralytic of whom the by-standers had just said jokingly: "The Brother must be pretty clever if he can heal that man." Some Protestants who were present exclaimed: "God is great!" That night the aged Brother came back from his office as if nothing unusual had happened.

The next day a religious observed, teasingly, "Brother André, it seems that two persons left your office in bad humor yesterday."

Knowing that he was alluding to the two sensational

cures, Brother André replied gently: "But you know that was not my fault; it was the fault of the good God."

Because he was imbued with this truth, the Wonder-Worker, even when he saw the crowds following him and showing him every mark of deep veneration, did not entertain the least sentiment of pride. "Not I, but God, or Saint Joseph did it." As a rule he was most reserved regarding the wonders he wrought. When urged to speak of the favors obtained through the intercession of Saint Joseph, he yielded, though reluctantly, and often used his sweet humor in the narratives. He always stressed the power of the Saint and when he perceived that he himself was an object of admiration, he would, in his own charming way, tactfully change the subject. When someone referred to the man cured of the palsy, he would retort: "Saint Joseph decided that he needs his two legs."

One day, after he had cured a cripple, an eyewitness asked him the man's name. Brother André replied that he had forgotten to ask him. The happy man, having deposited his crutches at the crypt, was going down the slope of Mount Royal at high speed. The inquirer ran after him, and, having overtaken him, asked him his name, and then came back to tell the Brother:

"His name is Laverdure."

"Well," said Brother André, "he has indeed grown green again."

Brother André saw God so visibly in these wonders that it was needless to preach humility to him. Once an Apostolic Delegate deemed it his duty to give him a little sermon on this subject; but he was told by the bishop accompanying him:

"Do not trouble him, for he would not comprehend your great precepts. Humility is his very life; he lives the virtue."

Another time, a canon was giving the Brother a long

exhortation on the dangers of pride. A man who was waiting impatiently to ask a favor interrupted the dissertation:

"Will you tell me which of you two is Brother André? I came from a long distance and I would liked to be cured."

The dignitary, startled at the indignity of being mistaken for a simple lay-Brother, retired, meditating on the vanity of dignities and the silliness of his own sermon.

★
★ ★

Further evidence of Brother André's humility is found in the fact that he accomplished the work of God without any concern for the esteem of others and without attaching any importance to the rank of those who came to him. His superiors and even bishops knelt before him to ask his blessing. He submitted with great reluctance to these marks of respect. When visiting the sick with a priest, he never complied with the request of those who asked his blessing, but invariably replied:

"It is your privilege, Father, to bless them."

Father Frederick, a Franciscan whose process of canonization has been introduced at Rome, came one day to the Oratory. "I have come," he said, "to ask Brother André what he is doing to become such a great saint."

The rector led him to the small chapel and ascended the stairs to the Brother's room. The latter came out to meet them. On seeing Brother André, the visitor fell on his knees, saying: "Give me your blessing, Brother André."

"No, Father Frederick, it is you, rather, who should bless me."

And there they were, each on his knees in a noble contest of humility. This edifying scene recalls the meeting of Saint Dominic and Saint Francis of Assisi. At length the little drama came to an end in a fraternal embrace.

The first meeting of these two men of God was not less touching. It happened early in the history of the Oratory. Yielding to the reiterated entreaties of a friend, the Reverend Father Provincial had allowed Brother André to join the annual pilgrimage of the Franciscan Fathers to Sainte-Anne-de-Beaupré. While Father Frederick was vesting for High Mass, the friend who had invited Brother André came to the priest and asked:

"Have you a server?"

"No, my friend."

"Then I shall present you with a server you will be delighted to see." He then introduced Brother André.

The humble religious was ever mindful of the great deference faith demands for a priest. At the breakfast table it was difficult to deter him from waiting on them while they, in their turn, tried in vain to serve him. When he met a priest coming from the altar, he fervently clasped his hand with deep reverence, for it had so recently held the Sacred Host.

"What can I talk about with a priest, I who am so ignorant?" he would often declare, for in his humility he did not realize how much he could teach a priest. Though he did not possess the learning of the philosopher or the theologian, he was endowed with wisdom of a higher order, mysticism, a direct knowledge of God. His narratives of the Passion of our dear Lord, which he could not recall without tears, enlightened one more than volumes of scholarly exegesis.

When called upon to meet persons of rank, he complied graciously and without false humility. Amiable of disposition and gifted with ready wit, he took a discreet and secondary part in the conversation without ever trying to monopolize it or to attract notice. Marks of unusual interest or of deference did not please him. He always sought the last place: in the refectory, the end of the table; in the church, the last stall, behind the altar.

His great detestation was to have his picture taken, and only the express command of his superior could make him consent. This explains his rather stern expression in most of his pictures when he was photographed alone. On the other hand, snapshots or group-pictures portray him naturally with his genial smile. In the early days of the Oratory he was ordered by the Father Provincial, the Reverend G. A. Dion, to sit for his picture, in two different poses. When the two proofs were shown him that he might select the one he preferred, he answered:

"It does not matter. The same dim-wit is shown in both pictures."

At his superior's request he sat twice before a renowned painter; but this command caused him so much distress that it was revoked and the artist had to finish the work from memory. Two months before his death he consented, though reluctantly, to have his bust executed from life.

A great personage came to see him one day and said: "I am the chaplain of the King of England. His Majesty knows of you through George Ham's book, *The Miracle Man of Montreal*, and he has requested me to visit you while on my journey."

The Brother listened absent-mindedly for a moment or so and then took leave of the visitor, saying: "There are some sick persons waiting for me at the office." The fact that this visitor was a man of importance and that he had come from a distance had no effect on Brother André.

Though he knew that there was perhaps no man in the country more widely spoken of than himself, he remained indifferent to fame. A Canadian who had lived in South America reported that the word Canada or Montreal was no sooner uttered than people inquired about Brother André. They might be ignorant of the names of Canadian bishops or public men, but they had all heard of Brother

André.

Those who came to the Shrine without confidence in Saint Joseph were quickly though politely dismissed. Those who were led by mere curiosity fared no better. Of such Brother André remarked: "It is very strange that some people come here without knowing why they come."

A lady who alleged as her reason for coming that she must be relieved of her fatigue, heard this reply: "Pray for me, for I, too, am very tired."

One could not attribute Brother André's humility to a blind unconsciousness of the honors and marks of veneration showered upon him, for praise always annoyed and displeased him. Endowed as he was with remarkable perspicacity, he readily detected any suggestion of it, and with his bright shield of humility he adroitly warded off all the shafts of vainglory. He felt that it was infringing on the rights of God and of Saint Joseph to arrogate to himself any credit for his cures. Without affectation, without sham modesty, he effaced himself from the foreground with the grace of genuine simplicity. In every detail of his life can be found that charming ingenuousness customary among saints, that naïveté which, far from being devoid of keen perceptive powers, is the fruit of the supernatural standard by which they do all for God, and attribute all blessings to Him, even to the extent of over-looking the fact that many around them are actuated by less noble motives. Thus it happened that Brother André, judging the world about him by his own sincerity, imputed all marks of deference to Christian courtesy.

To illustrate this point, we may cite an incident from his experiences when he took a trip to the United States. The parish priest who had the privilege of offering him hospitality contrived to give him the surprise of an official reception. A solemn procession of all the parishioners and public entertainment were some of the features. The

Brother, unaware of the fact that this demonstration had been in his honor, said to the rector on his return home: "I arrived at Jersey City just in time for a big celebration in the parish."

On another occasion, in travelling through Ontario, he once took the wrong train. The conductor, who saw by his ticket that he had made a mistake, told him to get off at the next stop. There the station master, full of solicitude, had him rushed to the nearest point where he could catch the fast train to Toronto. The train was signalled and the traveller got on, deeply impressed by such courtesy. Upon his return to the Oratory he expatiated upon the courteous attentions he had received, fully convinced that all travellers were recipients of like favors.

Always convinced of his own unworthiness, he shed bitter tears over the acts of impatience which he had inadvertently committed. In his dying moments he asked his fellows religious:

"Pray for my conversion."

The objection may easily be raised that since humility is truth, he could not fail to see that his spiritual life far surpassed that of those around him. Why, then, this disregard of his own worth?

Faithful to the teachings of Christ: "I have given you an example that you may do in like manner," he did not compare himself with other men. His only Model, his sole Ideal, was Christ Himself. We must not dismiss as mere childishness or scrupulosity his shedding copious tears over trifling faults; in his eyes all imperfections, however slight, marred his likeness to the Divine Exemplar. This conviction, which is common to all saints, harmonizes with the injunction: "Be you therefore perfect, as also your heavenly Father is perfect."

His ideal of sanctity was so high that he spurned all marks of veneration for himself, saying: "We keep relics of saints, not of persons like me."

In this matter he remained ever unyielding. Having learned that the Sisters carefully kept his old garments, he thereafter carefully counted every piece of his laundry and complained when anything was missing. As a precaution against being tricked, he burned all his worn-out clothes in the furnace.

During an interview with him, two Sisters cut off the tassels of his cord and carried them away in order to provide relics for their Community. When Brother André discovered his loss after their departure, he cried: "They are thieves. I cannot see how they can reconcile that action with their vow of poverty." And he asked that steps be taken to recover his property.

A faithful friend who attended the line of visitors at his office door used to ask them to pray in union with Jesus, Mary, Joseph, and Brother André. When the Brother heard this, he was visibly annoyed.

"Do not do that!" he said.

"But you pray every day for those who come to you. Have I not the right to ask them to pray in union with you?"

"Yes, provided you are not numbering me among the saints."

"There is no danger of that."

Brother André regained his composure, but he was very reluctant to allow the practice to continue.

Only for a supernatural motive, that of promoting devotion to Saint Joseph, could he be induced to appear before the public. On feast days when people came in crowds to the Oratory, he retired into solitude where, hidden from all, he took delight in seeing his great friend honored. Saint Joseph's little dog, as he styled himself, remained silent during the triumph of his master.

One can but think of Bernadette when she was asked: "Have you never had temptations to vainglory for having been thus favored by the Blessed Virgin?"

"What a strange idea," she replied. "Do I not know that the Blessed Virgin chose me because I am the most ignorant of mortals and that if she could have found one more ignorant she would have chosen her?"

Brother André, who was entrusted with a mission similar to that of Bernadette, had the same sentiments and made this answer to a like question:

"It is with the smallest brushes that the artist paints the most exquisitely beautiful pictures."

VIII

CHARITY

With forcible conciseness the prayer for the beatification of Brother André sums up perfectly the life of the servant of God: "Friend of the poor, of the sick, and of the afflicted." These titles, together with that of Apostle of Saint Joseph, denote his distinctive characteristics.

Jesus has established charity towards our neighbor as the special mark of His disciples: "By this shall all men know that you are My disciples, if you have love one for another."

Brother André possessed to an eminent degree this mark of the disciple of Christ. In meditating on his life we notice a continual efflorescence of deeds which bring to light the secret beauties of his soul, especially his heroic devotedness towards the sick. The following narrative by a happy beneficiary of this charity furnishes an instance:

"Saint Joseph's Oratory was in its infancy. I was in an extremely run-down condition. I could scarcely swallow even the light broth that was my only nourishment. I spat blood profusely at each fit of coughing. The doctors who were consulted told me that my case was hopeless and that I was a doomed man.

"But there was still one hope left for me — to see Brother André. While I painfully climbed the mountain I said to myself that I should come down either cured or in my coffin. The kind religious agreed to lodge me in a small room under the roof of the primitive chapel. Although this room was hardly large enough to accommodate one person, there was already another sick man there whose gangrened limb emitted an offensive odor. On the floor in a corner screened by hangings, the Brother had spread a thin mattress without sheets or blankets, and this he used for a bed. Every evening, though tired out from receiving pilgrims, he spent over an hour attending to us. Then, after extinguishing his light, he crept stealthily down the stairs which led to the chapel. One night I secretly followed him. By the dim light of the sanctuary lamp I saw him prostrate on the floor, absorbed in ardent prayer. Towards three o'clock in the morning he returned to rest on the hard couch he had reserved for himself.

"I had been at the Oratory for several days, but as yet there was no amelioration in my health. The dry cough and very difficult digestion persisted. One day the Brother served me at dinner a generous portion of meat and vegetables which he had himself prepared for me. He then ordered me to take a hearty meal.

" 'Brother André,' I said, 'if all the doctors in Montreal ordered me to do that, I would refuse but since you ask it, I will do your bidding, come what may.'

"I obeyed him, and was greatly surprised in the afternoon to feel better. At supper I was served even more copiously. . . . Within a few days I returned home perfectly cured, to the astonishment of my relatives and of the doctors.

"My companion still languished a long time. Several times he was on the verge of complying with the doctor's verdict that his leg should be amputated. I came to visit him occasionally. One day I brought with me a man who had forsaken his faith and whose conversion I eagerly sought. When he saw the hideous wound he crept away for fear of being overcome.

" 'If that man is cured, I shall believe,' he said.

"In the middle of November the sick man was suddenly healed."

Many such instances could be cited to prove the devotedness and self-forgetfulness of the little Brother. The following incident shows how earnestly he prayed to obtain the favors solicited by the sick. One evening at the hour when the lengthening shadows creep into every nook and corner of the deserted crypt to bring more into evidence the brilliance of candles and votive lamps, Brother André brought in a blind young man. Leaving the patient to himself, the Brother knelt and prayed, first on the pavement of the church, then on the steps at the railing, finally on the altar steps, halting on each step to pray.

A crippled young woman said to the Brother: "I have made a special trip from the United States to obtain my sister's cure."

"Why do you not ask for your own cure?"

"She is far more in need of health than I am; she has eight children."

"At this moment your sister is in perfect health. Now, think of yourself."

He took her crutches from her and made her walk. Overcome with joy at her cure, she wired the news to her sister and received this answer: "Obtained sudden cure."

On a stormy winter day a young woman whose limbs were totally paralyzed was rushed into Brother André's office during an interval when it was empty. Four persons accompanied her and at the Brother's request they all knelt to pray.

"Do you feel better?" he asked.

"I begin to feel a warmth in my limbs."

"That is a good sign, my child. Let us continue our ~ayer."

After a few moments he repeated his question.

"I feel an acute pain in my legs," she cried. Then she got up and began to walk. All continued to pray with tears of joy in their eyes.

Some of the cures recall the Gospel narratives. Towards the end of the Brother's life he suffered from heart trouble, and his doctors ordered him, when visiting the homes of the sick, to go to those only who lived on the first floor and to have those who lived on upper floors come down to him. One day as he was going along Bienville Street in Montreal, a sick woman was brought to him. Immediately all the sick of the neighborhood, children, men, and women were brought out until the whole street was filled with the sick and the infirm. Brother André attended to all with kindness, and his chauffeur when, after a long delay, he succeeded in starting and making his way through the crowd, remarked:

"How wonderful; it is like a scene from the life of Our Lord: everyone rushed forth to beg for favors and cures."

"Perhaps so, but God is surely making use of a very vile instrument."

This same thing happened many times. His friends asserted that they often had to ask for help to clear a passage for his car.

One day a man brought to Brother André's office his wife, who was seriously ill. Towards evening both retired to a small hotel nearby. During the night the woman had a very severe hemorrhage, and the doctor, who was immediately sent for, declared that she had only a few moments to live. Deathly pale and breathing almost imperceptibly, she seemed as one already dead. The doctor left, giving no sign of hope. The husband, however, impelled by his ardent faith, left his dying wife and ran to Brother André.

"My wife is dying, come and save her," shouted th

man, knocking at the Brother's window. The words sound like an echo from the Gospel: "Lord, my daughter is even now dead; but come, lay thy hand upon her, and she shall live." Again, "Lord, say only the word and my servant shall be healed."

Brother André dressed hastily, opened the door to his visitor, and led him to the crypt to pray at the foot of the altar surmounted by Saint Joseph's statue. After a few moments he said: "Go back to your wife. Do not worry; she will not die."

The man returned to the hotel and found his wife revived. She was saved. The next morning he called up the doctor to tell him the good news.

"You are joking; she is dead," replied the doctor, so sure was he that a return to health was impossible.

Brother André showed the same kindness to all without distinction, rich or poor, friend or foe. A certain doctor had relentlessly opposed him for several years with a zeal worthy of a better cause. One day his wife had a hemorrhage, and all the care given her proved of no avail. Her husband had recourse to the most learned of his profession but all was useless. Then the dying woman said to him:

"I wish to ask a favor of you. You must now realize that neither your knowledge nor that of other doctors can help me and that I am going to die. Get me Brother André. I beseech you to grant me this request."

The doctor hesitated between his self-love and his love for his wife. At last he decided to humiliate himself and went for Brother André. Scarcely had the religious crossed the threshold of the sick room when the hemorrhage ceased.

Following the example of Christ who, though sent to save the Jews, listened to the prayers of the Canaanite woman, Brother André obtained signal favors for those not of the Faith. All that he required of them was good

faith and confidence in God. The following story was related by a Protestant gentleman. His arm had been paralyzed for several years and doctors had attended him in
vain. At last he had recourse to Brother André, who said
to him.

"Since you have come to me, you must believe in Almighty God and have faith in miracles. I say to you:
raise your arm."

"I cannot; it is paralyzed."

"Raise it, I command you."

The man made the required effort and found that he
was suddenly cured.

One evening Brother André was having supper at the
home of a doctor, a friend of his. He inquired whether
there were any sick persons in the vicinity and was told
that there was a Protestant Englishman who had been
paralyzed for over a year and could not walk. In the evening the Brother went to see him and found him confined
to a wheelchair. He ordered him to get up and walk. An
old friend of Brother André who often accompanied him
was a witness to this cure.

While his devotedness in curing bodily ills was increasing, his zeal in curing moral ills was increasing still more.
As he said: "My greatest pleasure is to reconcile a sinner
to God." Knowing this, his intimate friends often brought
to him some hardened sinner, with whom he delighted to
talk or make the Way of the Cross. He loved the suffering
with all his heart, especially the spiritually weary, un-
believers, and adversaries of religion. He was deeply
grieved to see Communism seeping into Canada; and he
suffered and prayed because of it.

"Have you heard about the Communistic movement in

Montreal?" he inquired of his friends. As they tried to reassure him, he said: "It is when we hear nothing about the Communists that they are the most dangerous. I would not care if they put me to death by cutting me to pieces, provided the people do not suffer."

He had hoped for a long time to be put to death by the hands of Communists in order thereby to effect their salvation.

It was with the special purpose of winning souls to God that he went visiting the sick in the evening. To those who accompanied him he explained the spiritual good that was done on these occasions, to the sick, to members of their families, and to others who learned about these cures. On one such occasion, as he relates:

"At the request of a parish priest I went to visit a sick man who was an unbeliever and hardened sinner. On entering his room I asked him if he would permit me to rub him with a medal of Saint Joseph, since many, much sicker than he, had been cured by this means.

"The bed was very low and, as I knelt beside it, I suddenly felt him put his arms around my neck and draw me to him. I said to myself: 'I have you, my lad.' He was converted and died a holy death."

Rarely could a sinner resist the authority of the frail old man who, with tears in his eyes, talked about the Passion of Our Lord. Much could be written about his way of drawing hardened hearts to God. Ordinarily he took a crucifix from a drawer in his desk and began to speak about the Passion of Christ. He would relate all the details concerning the lashes and the pain of each wound, describing the lacerated flesh, and bones crushed by the nails. He would recall the ignominious insults of the Jews and the Roman soldiers, and would end his exhortation by expatiating on the infinite mercy of God. So earnest and sincere was he that he seemed to talk from heavenly inspiration.

At times he struck his audiences with awe; at other times he insinuated his ideas gently and persuasively into their minds. When he had moved his listeners to tears, he spoke of God's infinite goodness. How realistic was his presentation of the story of the Prodigal Son or of the Lost Sheep! He delighted in showing the artful and gentle way in which God's grace allures the sinner. He was most convincing when trying to awaken hope in sinners by recalling the conversion of some great sinner who, by becoming as ardent in loving God as he had been before in offending Him, grew to be a great saint. He often deplored the fact that we "do not insist sufficiently on the mercy of God."

But in preaching mercy he did not forget justice. Alluding to accidents and sudden deaths, he declared: "We must be always ready; the good God warned us that He would come like a thief in the night."

He knew how to make use of the most realistic comparisons in confuting erroneous opinions. To one, for instance, who declared that he had given up his religion because he had lost confidence in priests, he replied: "When you purchase something in a store, are you not indifferent as to whether the clerk who waits on you leads a good life or a bad one?"

Though he usually quoted the parables of the Master, he also composed some of his own to suit immediate purposes. A man who complained that his prayers were not heard and that he had even been severely tried immediately after making a novena to Saint Joseph, heard the following parable:

A man had three sons. That God might bless his family he came to the Oratory to make the novena preparatory to the feast of Saint Joseph. Shortly after the novena his eldest son fell sick and died. The following year he decided to make another novena. His second son took sick and died

The discouraged father swore that henceforth he would never pray. One day as he was going on a journey, his car was suddenly stopped. An unknown man accosted him and begged him to come into the neighboring forest. There the stranger showed him two corpses hanging from a tree and said: "Your two departed sons, had they lived, would have become assassins and thieves and would have ended their lives on the gallows. Your third son is destined to become a bishop. See what grief and affliction would have been yours, had I allowed them to live."

While recalling the teachings of Brother André, we regret our inability to express his tone of deep conviction and that tender look of his, so expressive of his unquenchable passion for doing good.

This benevolent charity imbued all his words. Usually he turned his conversation to serious topics, and everyone marvelled at the wisdom of his remarks. If the modern fashions were mentioned, he showed his firm stand against anything indecent. His experience with souls made him deeply resent those styles which the commercialized paganism of modern society, much to the degradation of the Catholic instinct of decency, continues to put on the market.

"If things go wrong," he stated bluntly, "it is the women's fault."

Through his close contact with people, he had become aware of the harm done to souls by immodest feminine attire. He had seen families disintegrated and the Christian education of children utterly neglected by frivolous mothers. He deplored the fact that our generation is un-mindful of modesty in clothing; and still more did he lament because he realized that the next generation would be paganized, not only in its outward apparel, but in its very soul.

He discerned the hidden causes of the apparently incomprehensible depression in business and industry. A few months before his death a friend asked him whether he thought the economic distress would soon end. He replied:

"No. God is angry because people do not pray. The depression is meant to teach the world a lesson. God is forgotten, many blaspheme against Providence and do not pray, churches are empty of worshippers. Economic conditions will change only when people pray more."

Brother André censured wrong only through duty, for by nature he was benevolent.

"Let us never give way to sadness," he often said. "Let us always be cheerful and avoid giving pain to anyone."

An inoffensive pun was his usual method of cutting short any words displeasing to God. "It is not always clever," he confessed, "but it puts a stop to uncharitable words, and God considers the intention."

He was exquisitely delicate in avoiding giving displeasure to others, and he knew well the art of complying with their unexpressed wishes. To please the Sister who had charge of preparing his meals he pretended, in spite of his bad stomach, to taste of every dish. A confrère who saw him nibbling at a biscuit said to him: "Ask for something else."

"Oh, no, it might cause the Sister pain."

He was very genial towards his friends. From the very beginning of his work they liked to gather round him for the Holy Hour and the Way of the Cross on Friday. He not infrequently took some of them to his room on Sundays to speak to them of the life of Saint Joseph and of the Passion of Our Lord. His friendships were genuinely supernatural, for, as he confided:

"We must become attached to God alone. I wish to

have no preference for anyone."

The poor and the afflicted, however, seem to have had a special claim to his sympathy. One of his friends remarked: "So long as I was in financial difficulties or worried about my health, I found him exceedingly kind. He was my adviser in all important business matters and always inquired about the outcome. I have often been in a position to see how much he respected, even venerated the poor and wretched who were the object of a special kindness on his part. When he saw them weeping, his pity was unbounded. He tried to turn their minds from their troubles and encouraged and comforted them. Not infrequently he tried to find work for the unemployed."

He requested his companions to bring sinners to him or to bring him to the bedside of the sick. During these charitable errands after office hours he stopped with some friends for supper, and showed them the most delicate kindness. Being informed on one occasion that one of his faithful companions was ill he went to see him, knelt at his bedside, and began to pray. Presently the sick man, who was at the point of death, opened his eyes.

"Well, how do you feel?" asked the Brother.

"A little better," came the feeble reply.

A few days later the patient, in perfect health, called at Brother André's office.

Another of his friends was to be operated on for a cancerous ulcer which was eating his thumb away. At the slightest touch the blood spurted out profusely. The Brother rubbed the diseased part a moment, and suddenly all trace of the ulcer disappeared. He then said jokingly: "The remedy you have been using relieved the pain for a moment; the doctor relieved you of your dollars; Saint Joseph has relieved you of everything." This story was related by Brother André to his nurse a short time before his death.

The following incident recalls the cure of Saint Peter's mother-in-law, whom Jesus healed on the occasion when He came to her home and found her sick with fever and unable to serve her guests their supper. So, too, Brother André came one day unexpectedly to the home of a doctor, a friend of his, and found the wife suffering from paralysis which had begun in one of her arms several weeks before. The Brother simply said to her: "At this moment you have no more pain in your arm."

The sick woman discovered to her joy that she was able to stretch out her arm and move it freely. When she got over her surprise, she served supper to her family and their distinguished guest.

A friend who had brought Brother André to the hospital to assist the victim of an accident said to him: "You have been playing tricks long enough, let me heal the sick person this time."

"All right," the religious replied, "I will take you at your word."

He ordered him to take off the dressing and to rub the sick man with a medal of Saint Joseph. The man was cured. On their way back Brother André whispered to his astonished friend: "Now that you have seen how merciful the Lord is, you will not in future have any doubts of His goodness to you."

While lavishing favors on his friends, he inculcated in them a love for suffering, after the example of Our Saviour, repeating often that we must not pray for exemption from pain but for courage to bear it generously, and giving examples from the saints who suffered martyrdom joyously.

"Be grateful to God for coming to you by trials, for you are very fortunate. If we only knew the value of suffering we would fall on our knees and with suppliant hands ask it of God."

To an old friend who told him about his troubles he

said: "Offer some prayers in thanksgiving to God, Who is looking after you."

"A queer way of looking after me, indeed."

"Do not talk like that. Later you will understand. God takes care of His friends and His best servants by sending them the cross. Suffering is of such great value that it can be fully rewarded only in Heaven."

For one so much given to works of charity as Brother André there might have lurked the danger of exteriorization of self to the detriment of the spiritual life; but in his charity we see the verification of the profound thought of the great mystic, Saint John of the Cross: "If our love for creatures is a purely spiritual affection, the greater the growth of this love the greater is our love for God, and the oftener the heart thinks of its neighbor the oftener does it think of God."

Charity! Charity! This was the counsel of the Master emphatically exemplified throughout His whole life. So, too, it is the counsel that guides the true imitator of Christ. But the doctrine of charity is, unfortunately, too often forgotten by those Christians who, in the struggle for life, prefer the ignoble motto: "Everyone for himself." Brother André incessantly preached the doctrine of love for the neighbor, and his lifelong practice of this evangelical virtue was the magnet that exerted on the crowds with whom he came in contact so powerful an attraction and influence.

IX

IMPERFECTIONS

Some of the biographies of saints are very misleading in that they are written without the conviction that personality is real. When saints are cleared of every imperfection and of every vestige of human frailty and portrayed in anaemic narrative as rose-scented types of mortals, they are unreal and unnatural. When such perfection is contrasted with the vivid reality of life, it is neither fascinating nor stimulating. Bernadette Soubirous, in whom we discover more than one trait of resemblance to Brother André, had a better understanding of sanctity:

"Saints are presented to us as perfect beings, without shortcomings, without failings, without inconstancy, without a single blemish. They appear to be so holy that we are disheartened at seeing ourselves so far from such a state of perfection."

God sanctifies the soul through the medium of human nature; and as human nature is never perfect but is prone to infirmities and frailties, an unrelenting struggle goes on between the natural and the supernatural. Brother André was no exception to this general rule; and it is with deep reverence and a sincere desire for reality that we delineate the slight imperfections that God left with His faithful servitor.

Though Brother André was one with whom converse was usually easy and agreeable, at times he was somewhat irascible, and more than one visitor was disconcerted at his seeming rudeness. However, while acknowledging that he frequently lacked patience, we must admit that this slight fault was more than counterbalanced by his heroic virtues. Then, too, an impartial study of his character will cause this apparent deficiency to diminish greatly in our eyes.

Far from displeasing God, Brother André seems rather to have been acceptable to Him even in his outbursts of temper. A Protestant lady who had come to his office was brusquely turned away. She went out weeping, but, as she stepped on the stairway, she realized that she was cured. She retraced her steps and threw herself at the Brother's feet to thank him.

An intimate union with God cannot admit of half-measures; the least attachment to sin paralyzes such a friendship, and hence Brother André vigorously combatted his irascibility, since he lived in such close union with God, Whose chosen instrument he was.

Without partiality or indulgence we may find excuses for his failings. He was of a nervous, even violent temperament. Left to himself as a homeless orphan, he was forced frequently to change his abode, and hence received practically no home-training and but a rudimentary education, not by any means sufficient to give him self-confidence or anything like polished manners. Yet with all these disadvantages he kept his natural tendency to irascibility in check until his resistance became weakened by advancing age and ill health. His occasional little explosions of irritation are explainable in view of the nervous strain incident to listening to human ills and miseries for more than five hours every day, and always standing, and the added tension of forcing his feeble, hoarse, almost extinct voice to make himself understood. At times his exhaustion was such that he spat blood. Those who knew Brother André before the ravages of illness had weakened him are unanimous in asserting that he received pilgrims from six o'clock in the morning until ten at night with the same unchanging affability.

Sometimes, with tears flowing down his withered old cheeks, he would confide to a confrère: "Alas! I have again made someone cry." Had the person whom he had rebuked seen him then, he would have been more tolerant and sympathetic. It is questionable whether he was fully responsible for losing his temper; in fact, when someone asked him one day whether he realized that he was doing so, he answered: "Not all all. I realized it only afterwards," and he was so utterly disconsolate that his confrères tried to console and cheer him.

God allowed these failings as a powerful antidote against pride and as a reminder of his frailty. When the Lord singles out a man to accomplish an exalted mission, He guards him with special care against the seductions of vainglory. Hence in God's elect souls the luster of sanctity is often eclipsed by some apparent weakness. It is well to keep this in mind that we may not misjudge Brother André.

At times his anger reminds us of that of Jesus against the buyers and sellers in the Temple. He was particularly irritated by persons who came to him through mere curiosity, and he rejected those who neglected prayer or who came to consult him as if he were a doctor, thus proving that his zeal was animated solely by the interests of God. Sometimes he declared: "I am not satisfied with myself; I have again been impatient. Ah! if the people could only realize that it is Saint Joseph alone who works cures!"

[113]

His angelic purity and his solicitude for the welfare of souls sometimes called forth sarcastic flashes of indignation. We here cite a few typical, satirical remarks which he flung at persons who appeared before him in unbecoming attire. A lady presented her daughter, a frivolous, much-painted young girl, saying:

"She is a good child."

"Is she your daughter? If I were you, I should not boast of it," came the curt remark.

Another lady who complained of a compression of the chest heard this sharp rejoinder: "It is surely not because your collar is too tight."

"Are you not afraid you will entangle yourself in your skirt?" he asked a lady whose dress was indecorously short.

With the keen insight of the saint he realized that the idolatry of style in dress, regardless of propriety, which makes it impossible to distinguish a Christian from a disreputable woman, was an abyss into which Christian civilization was being engulfed. To him who scrutinizes the moral evils springing from such levity and vanity no expression of condemnation is too forcible. Hence, we cannot reproach Brother André for his austere remarks on the evils and folly of indecent attire.

To be suspected of charlatanism aroused his indignation to the highest pitch. Once, when a blustering tourist asked him by what trick of hypnotism he healed the sick, he indignantly had the annoying fellow put out. He was not concerned about the personal insult, but he considered such insinuations an affront to Saint Joseph. His indignation was that of a son who sees his father insulted and treated with contumely.

By intuition he readily detected inadequate dispositions. Of a stranger who came into his office he said: "That man's prayer will not be heard because he has not a right intention."

A woman who kept a boarding-house and had lost all her boarders came, on the advice of a friend, to beg prayers from Brother André. His reply gave her a shock: "When you stop laughing at me and at the Oratory, your boarders will come back." Knowing how much she deserved the reproach, she later said: "I was so ashamed at seeing my sentiments known that I wished myself a hundred miles away from the Oratory."

In most cases his acts of impatience were acts of virtue in disguise made in defence of divine rights; and in other cases, could his reasons have been known, they would have redounded to his credit.

There are some who also reproached him with lack of religious regularity. God breathes the spirit of sanctity as He wills: some religious are remarkable for an edifying, lifelong punctuality in every detail and for exactitude in the observance of every point of the rule; others, on the contrary, owing to the requirements of their respective duties, may have to be a little inexact in Community regularity. The rule is a means of sanctification, not an end in itself. Our vision must be broad enough to recognize the designs of God when He promotes His end in diverse ways. The Lord has the right to sanctify His elect by any means He chooses. It is not merely the formal conformity to the rule which is important in the religious life. The conventual rule has a much deeper significance. There are many who follow the external observance throughout a lifetime without ever attaining an intimate union with God.

The apothegm, "a religious who observes his rule perfectly deserves to be canonized," is applicable not alone to he external observance, it applies also to fidelity to the spirit of the law — to the soul which gives it form. Brother André's way to sanctity was not that of the ordinary religious, but his way led him to a very high degree of virtue.

A burning love of God, with an ardent desire to make his whole life an exact copy of that of Jesus crucified, was the motivating principle of Brother André's life. Such love is pliant and all-embracing; it penetrates and vivifies every action; whereas the rule, followed to the letter in all its rigor without the spirit, leaves the soul superficial, cold, and languishing.

Ever actuated by the spirit of the rule, he conformed his conduct with entire submission to the will of his superiors. When he travelled, it was with the intention of doing good to others. Even the doctors themselves often asked him to visit and encourage their patients.

As a relaxation after office hours he sometimes went visiting those sick persons who could not come to him. This diversion was rendered necessary by his nervousness and his extremely fatiguing labor. His errant youth is indicative of his aversion to monotony. Those who were inclined to take scandal at his frequent calls on the sick would have done well to ask the opinion of the afflicted whom he comforted and cured.

It was hinted that he was too devoted to his evening calls. Quite frequently when his office hours were over, some friend took him to see the sick or the infirm, after which errands of mercy he would stop at the home of his friend, and return to the Shrine between nine and ten o'clock. With the approval of his superiors he sometimes went as far as Ottawa, coming back in the morning and resuming his work as if nothing had intervened.

In the course of his journeys he showed himself cheerful, affable, playful even, in order to gain everybody's favor and bring all nearer to God. After a few witty remarks, however, he gently gave the conversation a religious trend; and, once in his element, he talked with irresistible charm and simplicity. He took occasional holidays among friends or relatives, and at these times he made God and the things of God his constant topic of conversation.

Lest he should disedify his brothers in religion, he said to them confidentially: "You know it is not forbidden to travel in order to do good to our fellow men."

From his sojourns in the United States he frequently came back carrying crutches and other instruments used by the crippled whom he had healed there. At night he added them to the number of ex-votos already around the statue of Saint Joseph, in the manner of a brave soldier who brings to his chief war-trophies snatched from the enemy.

Far from being an obstacle to his sanctification, these outings rather added to it; hence the readiness with which his superiors granted these permissions, especially towards the end of his life.

He never interpreted the rule in a pharisaical spirit. If he spoke in times reserved for silence, it was for the purpose of doing good, of inspiring his fellow religious with the spirit of poverty, of charity, of love for God.

Whenever he did not assist at the Community recreations, it was because his work kept him away. Owing to the multiplicity of his tasks, he retired late but always with the permission of his superior. His sanctification demanded this sacrifice. When a priest reproached him with prolonging his prayers too much, saying: "You should rather offer your sleep to the Lord," Brother André replied: "You would not speak thus if you realized how much souls need our prayers."

He was right. Would he have attained the same degree of perfection if, after spending himself all day in the service of his neighbor, he had not devoted a part of the night to prayer? Saints, like men of genius, break away from the beaten path to follow one more arduous, thus allowing greater scope for the expansion of their God-given gifts.

The practice of offering one's actions to God is sometimes made a shield for the law of the least effort. It is not enough to offer one's life; there must be self-denial and love. Christians are only too prone to content themselves with a diluted form of renunciation; they too often mistake the shadow for the substance. They like to lead a life without hardships, a life of bounteous repasts, pleasures, and leisure, for the greater glory of God. Such a selfish, effortless existence cannot glorify God or be acceptable to Him.

Saint Margaret Mary, it is said, was of a very susceptible nature and became profoundly discouraged because her superior, she thought, no longer loved her. So too, one of the features of Brother André's personality was a marked tendency to susceptibility. He was, owing to his very impressionable nature, inclined to introspection and to a more or less veiled seeking of self. Despite his constant striving towards and progress in perfection, suffering and contradictions of all kinds had made him uncommunicative and even taciturn. A mere trifle was enough to break the ties of friendship, and the slightest indelicate or inconsiderate procedure grieved him. Some of his fellow religious, quite unintentionally, wounded him, and he suffered intense pain from their fancied disregard.

God, no doubt, willed matters thus for the more complete purification of his soul. If he had always been consoled by admiring confrères, he would have had but little merit. God wills that the road to sanctity be strewn with thorns.

It is related that Saint Margaret Mary was struck in the face for having dropped a dish on the floor while in ecstasy. Saint Thérèse of the Child Jesus on her deathbed overheard an aged nun saying: "What good has she don which may be told after her death?" So, Brother André, when he began his work, was persecuted, and even in his triumph, he found little consolation. It is remarkable that as soon as he became intimate with a confrère, some misunderstanding arose which chilled their friendship.

It matters little whether the trial was imaginary or real, he suffered as if it were a reality. He interpreted the reserved deference of his confrères as a sign of cold indifference. His advanced age and his sensitive nature account for this misunderstanding, which was permitted by Divine Providence for his sanctification. He even imagined, by misinterpreting an evasive gesture, that his superior laughed at him and considered him a fool. All these incidents were a source of much grief to him.

Theologians may object: "Then he did not live up to the doctrine of suffering which consists in submitting oneself lovingly to God."

It is easy enough to accept heroically the suffering of others, and to dilate on how others should bear up under tribulation. Although he was fully submissive to the will of God, Brother André sighed under affliction and wept like a child who thinks he is misjudged. We must not forget that grace embellishes, but does not destroy nature; and if it is engrafted upon a supersensitive nature, it makes it no less sensitive.

There are some who, imbued with a false spirituality, reproach him for complaining about his sickness or about unpleasant orders from his superiors. Does being a Catholic mean being a stoic? Must one deny suffering or ignore it? Brother André, who followed in the footsteps of Jesus, particularly in His Passion, knew that his Divine Model was not insensible to the sufferings His Father had inflicted upon Him. In spite of the fact that He was obedient even unto death, Our Saviour shed tears, besought His Father that the chalice might pass from Him, and yearned to open His Heart to His disciples. Although His soul was "sorrowful even unto death," He remains the Perfect Model of Obedience. Brother André, a disciple of Jesus Christ, well knew that the will of his superiors was the will of God, yet he suffered none the less from the rigor of certain injunctions.

He asserted repeatedly that God imparts extraordinary strength to the obedient religious. When He wants him to suffer, He allows superiors to be blind. "If, for example, we are already overburdened with work and we are requested to do more, we must accept willingly; we must always abide by the decisions of superiors. If we decline to accept the graces God has prepared for us, He will withold them from us. Nothing happens that God has not willed; we should never forget this truth. We must not do anything in opposition to the will of our superiors, not even the most useful things."

We may therefore say without hesitation that the few imperfections that are found in Brother André's life are far from being as striking as some might consider. They are rather signs of an authentic virtue, and they did not hinder him from becoming a living embodiment of our Divine Exemplar.

X

DEVOTIONS

PILGRIMS who come to pray before the black granite
tomb wherein the remains of Brother André are resting
so humbly may contemplate a painting by a great artist,
Henri Charlier, symbolizing the Brother's favorite devotions.([1])

The fresco in the center portrays the death of Saint
Joseph, to whose cult the venerable Brother had devoted
his whole life. Around the central group a border unfolds
in a free rhythmic flow produced by a succession of heavy
and light tones, full of Christian and calm serenity. It is
like a Gregorian melody transposed into colors, perhaps
an interpretation of the Requiem. It is a poem of colors,
rich and variegated, daringly and harmoniously blended,
showing a lively and luminous flight of imagination.

At first sight the devotion to Saint Joseph seems to
stand out pre-eminently in the life of Brother André;
but as one penetrates into his inner life, one sees that his
predominant devotion is to the sufferings of Our Lord.
Behind his tomb is painted a cross with the instruments of
the Passion grouped around it: the scourge, the nails, the
reed, the crown of thorns. So realistic is the fresco that one
feels the very force of the lashes lacerating the divine
Victim; the heavy crown is wreathed with green branches
not yet withered, and bent like bows ready to spring.

(1) Since a large chapel has been built behind the Crypt, where all
ex-votos are kept and where thousands of votive lights are burning
daily, the arrangement, as described here, has been slightly modified,
but the general picture remains the same.

From his early infancy Brother André had a very special devotion to Saint Joseph, and he made of him his close companion and his confidant during his wandering life as an orphan. He walked hand in hand with his great friend, who led him into a religious Congregation whose desire is to promote devotion to the Saint as the Patron of Workmen. He endeavored to have his brothers in religion, the pupils, the visitors, and the sick with whom he came in contact, share in this devotion. But great were the struggles he had to contend with, the obstacles to overcome, the sufferings to endure before his great work could be achieved and firmly established.

How well he described the life of Saint Joseph, chiefly in his sufferings! He was most solicitous to ascribe to him the miracles worked in his name and could hardly contain his indignation when some, neglecting to pray to Saint Joseph, cried out to him, "Heal me." He exacted an absolute, childlike confidence in that great Saint. An instance of this is found in the following prayer which he taught to one of his friends:

"O good Saint Joseph, grant me what you yourself would ask if you were in my place on earth, with a numerous family, and financial difficulties to overcome. Good Saint Joseph of Mount Royal, be my help, hearken to my prayer."

In his own estimation devotion to Saint Joseph could not be likened to devotion to other saints. Brother André, guided by the Holy Ghost, wanted his Saint to be honored widely as the Patron of the Universal Church. The underlying principle of this devotion was, that as Jesus was placed under the care of Joseph, so the Church, which is a continuation of Christ, must also be entrusted to his special care. He wanted to lay stress upon this doctrine: If Jesus remains the Sole Sanctifier, the never-failing source of all graces; if the Blessed Virgin, who came nearest to this supernatural source, being the Mediatrix of all grace, turns the course of that stream towards the earth, then Saint Joseph as the Protector of the Church is the steward who distributes the divine favors to men.

"It is owing to good Saint Joseph of Mount Royal," he liked to repeat, "that we have been safeguarded against Communistic revolutions in this country."

Brother André, in his discreet reserve, went to the grave with many undisclosed secrets about his intimate relations with the Patriarch whose representative he was on earth. The present sketch obliges us to pass rapidly over this particular devotion, which we have touched upon several times in our story.

★

★　★

In Brother André's life one thing stands out which at first sight surprises us, but which is, together with the miracles which he worked, the surest guarantee of his mission. Though he launched a prodigious movement of devotion to the Patron of the Universal Church, he spoke more willingly of the Passion of the Redeemer, the Mass, Holy Communion, and the inner life.

He often advised suppliants to make a novena to Saint Joseph, but he would add that the novena should be one of Communions, or Ways of the Cross. His private conversation dealt with the sufferings of Our Saviour so much that his friends recall numberless passages of such talks, whereas they remember hardly anything he said about the life of Saint Joseph.

Now and then he pointed out the perfect obedience of the laborer of Nazareth, his resignation in the midst of

[123]

trials, his sufferings and his joys; but he would soon resume his favorite topic: the love and mercy of God, redemption, Heaven. Then indeed he spoke from the bottom of his soul; his speech was as vivid as if he had witnessed the scenes he described, while tears flowed from his eyes as he spoke.

Another reason for his reserve with regard to Saint Joseph is that his devotion to him consisted mostly in an imitation of the virtues of the Saint. His mission was not to expound the hidden mysteries of the life of Saint Joseph, but, as appears from our narrative, to show himself a living copy of his protector.

Guided by the Saint, Brother André endeavored to make the devotion to his holy patron a first step towards God. He was radically opposed to that sentimental spirituality which fosters devotion to the saints but does not trace it to the source of the whole liturgical worship, namely, the Holy Trinity, through Jesus Christ Incarnate.

He had to strive against the ignorance of people who, unconcerned with living in the state of grace and loving God with their whole heart, came to beg temporal blessings from a friend of God as they would from a minister of state newly installed.

His conduct is an affirmation of this truth: if the Church requires that a special veneration be paid to the saints, to each according to hierarchical rank and to the supernatural favors imparted to him; if she weaves the liturgical year in great part with their office, still, all sacerdotal prayers, collects, secret prayers, prefaces, the canon, postcommunions, are addressed to the Trinity through Jesus Christ; and the secondary formulas, the prayers addressed to the saints, are so many channels draining into the great liturgical stream which flows into the ocean of the Divinity.

In worship of the Holy Trinity Brother André made use of an intermediate devotion to the Blessed Virgin, especially to Our Lady of Sorrows. He learned from Saint Joseph to go to Jesus through Mary. Since this is but a brief sketch, we shall merely note in passing his love for Mary, which devotion is a necessary condition to divine action in the soul.

Sanctity consists in practising to a high degree the virtue of charity — Jesus Suffering is the door to this intimate union with the Trinity.

The life of a lay Sister of the Order of the Visitation, Marie-Marthe Chambon, had, on account of her special devotion to the Blessed Wounds of Our Saviour, a marked attraction for Brother André. A nun who came frequently to see him brought him a biography of the nun. He was so delighted with this life, which resembled his in more than one respect, that on her next visit he said: "I want eighteen copies of this life — to convert eighteen sinners."

"You surely do not mean that, Brother André. I do not have them, and they are not to be found in Montreal."

"That does not matter; I must have them."

The Sister departed, a little vexed with the whim of the religious. When she reached her convent and went to the library, she found two dozen copies of the book she had wanted, carefully wrapped up. No one in the house could tell her where the books came from.

For a long time Brother André had been putting into practice the counsel given by Jesus to the humble Visitandine nun:

"Do not turn your eyes away from My Wounds; they are a book from which you will derive more knowledge than from the most learned man. Everything is contained in prayer to the Sacred Wounds."

He learned from that book the Rosary of the Sacred Wounds, in which there is substituted for the Ave Marias this supplication: "Through the merits of Thy Sacred Wounds, my Jesus, pardon and mercy." He did his utmost to propagate this devotion.

The sufferings of Our Redeemer became his absorbing love and his constant preoccupation. The Passion was always his favorite topic of conversation. He liked to enter into detailed descriptions such as we read of in the prophets or the mystics; his whole life was influenced by this constant turning of his mind towards the Passion of Christ.

"In order to pray well," he declared, "we must think of Jesus on the Cross. Is it possible to have distractions when one sees his Brother crucified?"

He showed the greatest respect for the representations of the Passion. All were impressed by the reverence with which he saluted the wayside crosses and lovingly gazed upon them. During the Holy Hour or Benediction of the Blessed Sacrament he would remove the veil of the monstrance if placed over the crucifix, and put it on the credence table. "The image of Jesus Crucified must not be used as a stand," he would observe when the service was over.

Entering a house one day, he remarked: "Your home is well furnished; there is only one thing wrong."

"I should like to know what it is, Brother André."

"A very serious mistake: Jesus does not hold the first place," he said, pointing to a crucifix hanging on the wall, in a corner.

His piety made him delight in reading the writings on the Passion by Saint Gertrude and saintly Catherine Emmerich.

Were this chapter not limited to the study of the highlights of Brother André's soul, it would be very interesting to dwell on his devotion to the Holy Eucharist. It was with a trembling hand that the priest approached him at the moment of Communion to give the Sacred Body of the Master to him whose face brightened up so suddenly in his silent and loving expectation. How well he knew how to find forcible expressions to encourage frequent Communion!

"If you stayed a long time without taking any nourishment how could you live? If you do not go to Holy Communion, you cannot remain long in the state of grace."

His comparisons were strongly realistic. "What would your wife say if you were a whole month without showing her any marks of affection? She would say that you do not love her. You would cause trouble in your home. Well, when you do not receive Communion God says to Himself that you do not love Him. And there is trouble in your soul."

"Before Mass," he recommended, "always say this prayer: 'O holy Angels, grant that I may be filled with the presence of God on the altar as you are penetrated by it in Heaven.'"

His love of the Holy Eucharist was impregnated with a love for the sufferings of the Master; the Holy Hour which he inaugurated at the Oratory every Friday evening was followed by the Way of the Cross.

The saints, in their deep inner life, have their individual traits. They are not moulded in one form as the plaster statues in our churches; each one is a unique work of the Divine Artist. What chiefly characterizes Brother André's piety is the close relation between the devotion to Saint Joseph and that of the Passion; this was the main point of his spirituality. While making the Stations of the Cross he seemed to be conversing with Saint Joseph. When he was ill he performed that pious exercise holding his crucifix in front of the statue of the Saint.

Nothing is more natural than to link these two devotions. Assuredly God, Who sculptures the souls of His elect with the rude chisel of suffering, did not spare Saint Joseph from that sword of sorrows whose sharp point lacerated the heart of the Blessed Virgin. Joseph who, with Mary, prepared the Divine Victim had, during his whole life, forebodings of the great sacrifice; the Passion filled his loving heart. A bas-relief which it is planned to place at the beginning of the Way of the Cross on the mountain, contains a summary of the Brother's spirituality; Saint Joseph is giving his hand to his apostle to lead him along the sorrowful way.

His devotion to the Patriarch of Nazareth, directed towards the suffering humanity of Jesus through Mary, reaches the Trinity in a perfect cycle. He frequently recommended prayers to the Holy Ghost and he had a great devotion to Our Lady of the Holy Ghost. Docile to divine inspiration, he followed the normal sequence of the liturgical worship: Joseph, Mary, Jesus Suffering, the Trinity, Father, Son, and Holy Ghost.

Another distinguishing mark of his spirituality is its stamp of his formation as a laborer. He attained sanctity not as a learned theologian but as a lay-brother. We find instances of this in his love for vocal prayers and simple external practices of devotion adapted to the understanding of the common people, such as novenas, devotion to the Seven Sorrows and the Seven Joys of Saint Joseph, the Rosary of the Sacred Wounds, mounting the stairs up to the Oratory on his knees, and reciting Aves.

This simple method of an intimate union with God must be carefully noted; it shows that sanctity is a duty for all and is accessible to all. To overlook that aspect would be as great a mistake as that of the cold academic artists who, under the pretence of beauty, represent the Artisan of Nazareth with the dignity of a Greek philosopher or of a Roman emperor instead of depicting his spiritual life under the features of a workman.

Numerous and varied as they were, Brother André's religious exercises did not encumber his spirituality. He was always animated with the liberty of the children o'

God. A multitude of pious practices soon hampers the lukewarm but it stimulates the fervent, just as a bundle of faggots will extinguish a dying flame but kindle a blazing fire.

When Brother André began his first chapel he often spent whole nights conversing with God. One of his friends revealed:

"Frequently, after his sick calls, he invited me to sleep in his cell over the primitive chapel. More than once I struggled against sleep in order to watch him. Towards morning I fell asleep while he remained in prayer. When I awoke, about five o'clock, I often noticed that his bed had not been touched."

As he grew older, one would not expect him to be able to spend the whole night without sleep, yet, until a very advanced age, a few hours' rest seemed enough for him. Oftentimes he had no sooner retired than he immediately got up again to spend the remainder of the night in prayer.

Those who witnessed these long watchings were amazed at seeing him cheerful and alert in the morning. One of them reports: "During the summer of 1936 I had the good fortune of receiving him as a guest for some time. He was quite unwell. Severe attacks of angina threatened to carry him off. Habitually he retired at nine o'clock, but at about eleven o'clock he arose to pray and read until morning. I invariably expected to find him exhausted after a sleepless night."

"How are you?" I inquired when he appeared.

"I feel fine," he would reply.

Indeed he was really refreshed. Prayer seemed to rest him as much as sleep.

All through his life the evening, after his sick calls, was the time he devoted to his intercourse with God. When the doors of the church were closed, he went alone r with a few companions into the deserted nave dimly

[129]

illumined by the flickering flames of the vigil lights.
There in the odor of incense and burning wax, he pondered
over the woes with which he came in contact. He prayed
for all those for whom he had promised to pray: one decade
of his Rosary for such and such a sinner; one decade for
such and such a sick person. Prayer was perceptible on
his lips and in the expression of his face. Those who caught
a glimpse of him learned what prayer is like when there
is something behind the words pronounced. Only when
completely tired out did he bring his colloquy with God
to a close.

Nearly every evening of the year 1927 an employee of
the Oratory was witness to these long communings with
God!

Kneeling on the hard floor, near the Communion rail
in front of the high altar, Brother André spent an hour,
with clasped hands, motionless, plunged in contemplation.
Then he made the Way of the Cross, quite unlike our
precipitate and distracted performance. At each station
he knelt a long time. He seemed to undergo the tortures
of the Passion, so contracted were his features by the pain.
He took nearly an hour to go round the church. His
robust companion had to confess himself outdone by the
old man, and remained sitting in a pew.

Wonderful things happened during these long talks with
God.

As the Brother himself confessed, his recollection was
so deep that his companion could leave him or walk in the
church without his noticing it. One evening as he thus lay
prostrate in the center aisle, the statue of Saint Joseph,
becoming suddenly resplendent in the darkness, seemed to
advance towards him on a trail of luminous clouds.

Awe-stricken and bewildered, the man shook Brother André but could not distract him from his prayer. He hastened out of the church pale and trembling and told the incident to the first religious he met. He was brought to the Father Rector and again related the apparition, declaring himself too excited to go back into the church that night. The religious attached no importance to the affair in spite of the reiterated protestations of the witness: "I was not asleep, and I'm not insane. The apparition lasted about three minutes. I could not be so upset if it were all fancy."

On another occasion when Brother André had remained in his stall behind the altar late at night, a bright light shone suddenly in that part of the sanctuary where he was kneeling.

Three or four different times a star-like fire shone over his head while he was making the Way of the Cross. Very often a personage seemed to accompany him from station to station. Absorbed in his prayers, the Brother did not take heed of the phenomenon. His companion looked all over the church without discovering any hidden person; as soon as he approached Brother André the personage vanished. Could an explanation of this strange fact be found in the characteristic prayer of Brother André, uniting devotion to Saint Joseph with that of the Passion? Did the Patriarch of Nazareth come to converse with him in order to help him to fulfill his mission?

Some will perhaps say, "This is the vagary of an over-wrought imagination." But the account comes from a man of mature age, a laborer who had nothing mystical about him. God ordinarily allows us to catch a mere glimpse of the marvellous in the lives of the saints. He saves them from indiscreet inquiries, allowing, at the same time, certain signs to appear in order to insure their triumph after death.

Brother André himself narrated an apparition which was immediately taken note of by a Father at the Oratory. On September 28, 1931, the Brother was going to bed when his eyes were struck by the sight of a luminous, heart-shaped picture. He thought himself in the presence of Our Lord; but, in his earnest desire for truth, he confessed he could not assert this with certainty. A few moments later he perceived distinctly the Blessed Virgin with the Child Jesus in her arms. Seeing her advancing towards him, he sat up on his bed, exclaiming several times, "My Mother, O my Good Mother!"

Later on, he related the same apparition to another priest, imitating all the gestures of the miraculous personage.

Let us pass rapidly over these extraordinary events. God permits these mystical phenomena to occur frequently in the lives of certain saints, whereas with others He does not want these to predominate. The humanly inexplicable success of Brother André's work, his life of prayer, of self-denial, of sacrifice, as well as the innumerable wonders he worked, remain the best proof of his mission.

We have given here but a brief sketch of the apostle of Saint Joseph. We deeply regret that he himself did not, as did little Thérèse, delineate the hidden workings of his soul. God seems to have reserved for Himself the direction of his spiritual life and to have purposely concealed its beauties, letting only the grandeur of his mission become known.

XI

SPIRITUAL LIFE

Wᴇ ʜᴀᴠᴇ now reached the last stage in our onward journey through the avenues of Brother André's soul. After a brief portrayal of his life, we have attempted to bring out the virtues notably expressive of his holiness: his confidence, his humility, his charity. We have also pointed out the shadows in the picture and, before entering within a sphere less perceptible to the senses, we have mentioned his devotions or the apparent characteristics of his inner life. Let us now leave off the externals and investigate the soul of his sanctity.

When we consider a truly inspired work of Christian art; for example, the angel frescoed where Brother André's tomb was previously located, we readily seize the design, the outlines expressive of Christian thought, but we ask ourselves what else there is in the painting that brings out such a keen sense of the presence of God and of the Beatific Vision, whereas hundreds of similar works done with equally meticulous care do not give even a suggestion of the supernatural. Something more than the technical ability of the painter must account for the difference; and that something is inspiration. We, on our side, can read the idea of the artist in his work only in so far as our minds rise to his level.

A saint is a masterpiece of the Divine Artist; to perceive

the exterior lines of his life is easy enough, but to grasp the rhythm which animates the drawing and gives it its supernatural character is more difficult. We can penetrate to the intimacy of his soul only in so far as we rise by a living and enlightened faith to the height of the divine idea and the invisible action of God in the soul.

A saint is not a listless being, but one animated with spiritual life. To understand him, therefore, we must grasp his intense interior life in all the beauty of its steady growth and forward movement. Our intellect has a tendency to regard as static all that it considers — to detach a few notes instead of grasping the changing melody as a whole. The spiritual life requires a continual growth of the soul enriched by divine grace; it is grace itself being lived, charity being practised, a masterpiece being developed.

The criterion by which the Greeks judged the perfection of a work of art was the masterpiece of some great artist, renowned for its proportions, its harmony, and its expression of intellectual and religious truth. The canon of spiritual beauty is Christ, the Masterpiece par excellence, the Artist and the Work, God and Creature; and we study the saint in his likeness to Christ.

Every Christian is, likewise, at the one time, instrument and artist; God does not operate in the soul without the co-operation of our free will which, by constant effort, attempts to make an exact copy of the Divine Model. The only end and justification of our existence is the reproduction of the life of Jesus in our lives, thus making of them another Gospel.

★
★　★

It is interesting to study Brother André as an artist — to find out how he learned to know and imitate his Model. He acquired all his knowledge by constant reading and

by meditating on the Gospels. All his teaching is derived
from that source. When we question those who were fortunate enough to receive his counsels, we get a unanimous
answer: all declare that he won them by means of the
Gospel, surpassing preachers in his ability. All his doctrine
was drawn from the Passion and the Parables.

Far from being disheartened by the stern teachings of
the Gospel which we so often spurn, he sought in Christ
crucified a rule for his life. Some great saints have confessed that they were led astray in the beginning of their
spiritual life because they aimed directly at a union with
the Trinity. Brother André, guided by Saint Joseph in his
ascent towards God, was well aware that the point of contact with the divine world is the suffering humanity of
Jesus. Such sound conduct was due to the guidance of the
Holy Ghost, Who instilled into his soul the gift of supernatural wisdom and supernatural understanding, which
guided him towards the enjoyment of the Incomprehensible. The assertion that the knowledge of Christ is
due not to natural talent but to divine inspiration is no-
where more evident than in Brother André's life.

He had another favorite book: *The Imitation of Christ*.
In his leisure hours he enjoyed reading those pages so
redolent of the Gospel. Often he was found absorbed in its
perusal. A nun who once paid him a visit expressed her
astonishment at seeing him use a book printed in such small
type, and asked him: "Brother André, how can you read
that print? I certainly could not."

"It is quite easy. Read this page."

"Impossible, I have broken my glasses and I can hardly
see clearly enough to find my way about."

"I want you to read it."

The nun complied, and was quite amazed at being able
to read without difficulty. When she left the office and
found herself again shortsighted, she said to her companion:

"It is wonderful that I was able to read that book!"

Brother André read it so often that he knew it almost by heart. He liked to explain to religious the chapters concerning the inner life, and to comment on the manner of keeping the thought of God in mind even in the midst of the most absorbing occupations.

Another source from which he acquired his knowledge of God was the lives of the most faithful disciples of the Master. He delighted in reading the biographies of saints. He assimilated all he read about them and in conversation pointed out innumerable passages from these books. Those who thought him ignorant of spiritual things because he had not received a liberal education were soon undeceived. He discussed with ease matters of the deepest spirituality and expressed very broad views on the subject. When he perceived that he was not understood, he made himself clear by means of most realistic comparisons.

Not in books only did he obtain his knowledge of God, but even more by close contact with Him Who inspired the sacred texts. He never missed an opportunity of recommending prayer to the Holy Ghost, Whose divine lights inundated his soul.

"What the Holy Ghost did for the Apostles," he declared, "He will do for us."

His supernatural knowledge was reflected in his entire life. That his zeal was modelled on the apostolate of Jesus is very obvious, as we have shown in every page of this book. But he applied himself with the same care to reproduce in his soul the interior life and the renunciation of the Master.

Towards the end of his life, he remarked: "I have asked God to keep me always in His presence, like the saints in Heaven."

How close a union with God is manifested by this desire of leading a heavenly life here on earth! This habit of living constantly in a world of faith explains his power of moving sinners to repentance. His knowledge of Jesus Suffering led him to a loving understanding of the Trinity, which is the very foundation of the Christian life. Heaven is, indeed, the blossoming of this knowledge of our faith into the Beatific Vision. The true life, the only one that had any importance in his eyes, was that which is a foretaste of our eternal home. This explains why he already seemed to live there. His intimate friends, who often heard him speaking of this celestial abode, declared: "When he described Heaven, he seemed to see it, so brightly did his countenance beam with joy."

During the last years of his life especially, Paradise became his favorite subject of conversation and he would spend hours describing its beauties. On several occasions he declared: "Only a veil separates us from God."

He was anxious to tear off that veil: "You know," he said, "it is not forbidden to desire death in order to be with God."

A person who heard him picturing the beauties of Paradise, observed: "None the less, we are all afraid to die."

"When we have lived a good life," he replied, "we need not fear death, which is the door to Heaven."

"Yes, but Heaven is so far away."

"The distance between Heaven and earth is so short that God always hears us."

And the better to persuade his friend, the Brother recited, in a voice so low that the syllables were scarcely audible, the Our Father and the Hail Mary. "You see," he went on, "God hears me, which proves that Heaven is not so far away."

Long since, he had given up the childish notion that Heaven is a kind of enclosure which we enter after death. His entire life is a constant reminder that Heaven, being a penetration into the Deity, must be lived by faith while we are behind the veil that screens the supernatural world from our eyes. As the light of the Holy Ghost filtered more and more into his soul, he became more familiar with this truth which ruled his whole life.

He dearly loved to meditate on the things of God. Sweet visions, divine colloquies held him kneeling for hours, his eyes half-closed, his heart centered on the secret beauties hidden in his soul. Any attempt to disturb him in those moments showed how deeply he was immersed in prayer and lost, for the time being, to all other considerations. Only a grave reason could determine him to sacrifice these precious moments. The tone of his answer to one who insisted on bringing him to the sick shows this: "What are you thinking of? I cannot leave my prayers!"

His prayer was not that of a spoiled child who wants to obtain something from his father, nor was he miserly with God. He never made bargains in his prayers by asking a favor when he did anything for God. He never confused asking with giving, nor giving with asking.

Touching indeed was his prayer before the Blessed Sacrament for all the nations of the world. Great is the breadth of Catholicism, which unites in the same thought the Pope, the great white-haired old man, looking at the world with fatherly eyes from the Eternal City, and the little old man praying for the same intentions on Mount Royal.

Brother André's spirit of prayer developed in him a profound spiritual life, an intimate knowledge of Christ and, through Him, of the Holy Trinity. Remembering the Gospel warning: "Without Me, you can do nothing," he prayed like a child imploring his mother; he wept, proclaimed his unworthiness, spoke heart to heart with his Lord. He tended with his whole soul towards God, Who returned his ardent love by enlightening his intellect. God loves a complete self-surrender. He wants an unconstrained yearning of the soul towards Him in the free, spontaneous love of a caressing child whose life gravitates towards Him as the magnet to the pole. In the midst of agitations and disturbances, Brother André invariably kept close to God by His burning desire, which was an unspoken prayer. The remark of one of his friends: "He seems to be attracted toward God as toward a magnet," is expressive of his whole life.

The vigor of God's action in his soul was manifested by his zeal for the sanctification of others. He neglected no opportunity of turning the conversation to religious subjects. His friends often said: "He used to begin with some trite remark and then, in his own inimitable way, turn the talk to God."

He strove to imitate Christ, not only by a life of continual prayer, but also by an unceasing abnegation of self, for he was convinced of the necessity of renouncing every attachment in order to live closely united to God.

"Remember," he insisted, "that if we wish to be good Christians, we must not be attached to the world."

He himself was ready for any sacrifice. A few months before his death, thinking that his superiors wanted to send him away from the Oratory, he confided the following to a friend: "I am not of much use now at the Oratory; perhaps I am only doing harm here, for I am becoming very old. If my superiors decide to give me another occupation at the next appointments, I shall be satisfied, so long as I am of some use to the Congregation. Perhaps God wants that sacrifice of me before I die. After a little rest I shall feel strong enough to do some other work."

Truly was great renunciation required, thus to look seriously upon the possibility of a sudden change of obedience and to be ready to suffer an injustice which would mean a public disavowal of all his glorious past!

His anticipated vision of Heaven gave him courage to

follow Christ along the road of sacrifice. He could not, on account of his weak constitution, impose severe macerations on himself, yet he was very mortified. All during his life of patient drudgery and continued sickness he retained that ardent desire of imitating Christ Crucified which had impelled him during his youth to inflict corporal penance on himself. He mortified himself unsparingly by nightly prayer and severe labor, by allowing himself, during the forty years of his stay at the college, only a few short hours of sleep on a pallet or on a mattress placed on a board. He asked for no help, but was content to accept what was given him. He took his food, in preference, without seasoning. In his extraordinary frugality he was satisfied with an unappetizing food, made of a mixture of flour and water. Smoking, newspapers, the radio, all amusements were unknown to him.

Let us not suppose that such detachment cost him no effort. Brother André was sensitive and affectionate. He had a great love for nature, for flowers, for children, and for his friends, but that was nothing compared to the Great Love which consumed his whole life.

In order to resemble his Divine Model he practised the most rigorous poverty. When he was doorkeeper he had to be neatly dressed. Once, perceiving that his cassock was no longer fit to wear, as it was threadbare, patched, and faded, he whispered to a young day-student who often mailed letters for him:

"I heard that your mother often does sewing for the poor."

"Yes, she does," replied the boy.

"Would you ask her if she could make me a new cassock from two old ones?"

Delighted at the idea of doing something for "Good Brother André," the lady came to him and said: "Don't bother about your old cassocks, I shall find some, for I know that the ones you have are not fit to be used again."

Some time later, arrayed in his made-over cassock, he received the charitable dressmaker in the parlor and, smiling, said: "I got caught, all the same; the Brother-bursar recognized pieces of his coat."

He was always scrupulously observant of his vow of poverty. For the sake of that virtue, even in his old age, when he came home from his sick calls at night, he examin-ed the doors and windows to assure himself that they were properly closed, and saw to the extinguishing of all the lights.

He spent millions of dollars for the glory of Saint Joseph and the welfare of laborers, and yet he himself lived like a poor man. He liked to style himself Saint Joseph's little dog. He never received or gave away the least thing without the permission of his superiors.

Naturally, he did not acquire such a degree of renuncia-tion in a short time. "Do not forget that sanctity does not come all of a sudden," he said to a confrère towards the end of his life.

In the spiritual as in the natural order, beings grow by dint of self-denial, by the death of the seed that gave them birth, by assiduous care, by abundance of water and light; they never spring forth spontaneously. Spiritual consola-tions are rare accidents. The law of spiritual progress calls for the sacrifice of all that is natural, and obedience to this law is absolutely required if we want to live in union with God and obtain eternal bliss. This is the manner in which Brother André increased in virtue. In addition to continual bodily ailments and contradictions of all kinds, he suffered certain trials very similar to the sufferings of Christ. We shall quote one such fact transmitted to us by an eye-witness. Towards the close of his life, after an illness which almost carried him off, he was permitted to spend a few days of convalescence at the home of one of his intimate

[141]

friends. There he had a relapse and had to be taken to a hospital. The ambulance men, inured to suffering, ruthlessly placed him on a stretcher and motored him downhill, head first. One of them remarked mockingly: "He who has healed so many others cannot heal himself!" This sounds like a repetition of the blasphemous words of the Jews: "He saved others; Himself he cannot save."

Who can describe the deeper suffering of his heart so enamoured of divine love when God suddenly withdrew all sensible consolation, leaving his life darksome and burdensome! Ah, what distress was caused by the apparent absence of the Great Friend who had suddenly disappeared in the dark night, carrying away with Him all the light of his soul and all its nourishment! What loneliness he endured during those dismal hours when the Friend for Whose sake he had given up everything and Whom he passionately loved, had forsaken him! No trial is greater than this abandonment which caused Our Saviour Himself to say: "My God, My God, why hast Thou forsaken Me?"

★
★   ★

As we contemplate the beauty of this soul thoroughly moulded by the light of the Gospel and direct personal contact with the inspired texts, we realize the mighty influence of the Sacred Scriptures on the faithful. The Gospel endows one with a sharpness of penetration which the most advanced studies cannot impart. We are struck by the light of understanding the life of Christ that God gives to the humble who go to Him in the simplicity of their loving hearts and with none of the cold impersonal curiosity of intellectuals. We are inclined to forget our poverty and need and, instead of raising suppliant hands to God, we look upon ourselves as rightful owners of the treasures of faith. Hence, while the saints partake of the banquet of the Sacred Books, we pick up the crumbs.

Brother André stands out as an extraordinary figure in our times; for we are living on the ruins of Christian civilization, in a world which, under the mask of Christianity, does not reproduce even the essential outlines of the figure of Christ. Christians are forgetting the law of the love of God which precludes all love of the world: "Be ye perfect as also your heavenly Father is perfect." Their ideal is lowered to the state of those who know nothing of the supernatural order. They strive simply to avoid mortal sin. They forget that Christ has identified true love of God with a contempt for those things which are good and desirable from a natural point of view only. "If any man love the world, the charity of the Father is not in him. No man can serve two masters."

Too many Christians are obstinately set upon trying to conciliate two things which are incompatible: fulfilling the precept of loving God with their whole heart, with their whole soul, with their whole strength, and at the same time reserving a part of this strength, of this soul, and of this heart for the world with its pleasures, its luxuries, its licentiousness. They desire the precious pearl and the hidden treasure spoken of in the Gospel, but they will not purchase it with the sacrifice of all their possessions. Many who pretend to know Christ, know Him merely as one knows a stranger. Yet, He is a Friend, a Model which they should reproduce in themselves to the extent of being able to say with Saint Paul, "I live, now not I; but Christ liveth in me."

They subconsciously minimize the essential part of the life of Christ; that is, His Passion and His Cross. But few follow to the letter the invitation of the Master, "If any man will come after Me, let him deny himself, and take up his cross daily and follow Me."

We picture to ourselves a Christ after the manner of the Jews, who selected in the prophets those traits that flattered their passions, and left aside the characteristics that ran counter to their own desires. We dream of a Christ Who suits the measure of our natural inclinations. We look upon Him as a Model Who approves of luxury and comfort, one Who tolerates worldly maxims and material pleasures, and meanwhile we satisfy our conscience with an occasional aspiration towards Him.

A Christian revolution has become a necessity not only among Communists but among Catholics as well. We must revert to the spirit of the first Christians, for too great indeed is the distance between us and the Divine Exemplar, between the Gospel of our lives and that of Christ. Not without reason have we made this digression. It does not suffice to narrate the events in the life of Brother André; we must tell our story in such a way that it will be fruitful for souls. If we study Jesus as a Model to be reproduced in our lives, so must we study the man who is a copy of Jesus — another Gospel of Christ.

The Church prudently reserves the right of officially crowning the virtue of her saints. With the greatest respect for the decision of Holy Church, we wish simply to state that Brother André already appears to all as a Model for imitation.

In his lifetime Brother André would have liked to sculpture a whole nation to the likeness of the Crucified; since his death he wants to readjust a whole nation to the measure of Christ. To him may be applied the words which Paul Claudel in his *L'Annonce faite à Marie* puts on the lips of one of the characters, old Anne Vercors, who is leaving for a pilgrimage to the land sanctified by the Passion of Christ: "The whole kingdom is directed and attracted with me to the throne of God, and is regaining its sense of direction towards Him. I, as the deputy, carry

[144]

it with me to fashion it anew on the Eternal Pattern."

The life of Brother André is not merely a virtual reflection of the radiant figure of Christ, but a real, con-
temporaneous, masterly reproduction of the Divine
Exemplar. Because we are all called to a high development
in the Spiritual Life, we must insist on the positive obliga-
tion of striving incessantly to reproduce the life of Christ
in ourselves; and to effect this purpose we must have a
great esteem for the heroes of virtue. Between the sanctity
of persons worthy of being exalted by the Church and that
of ordinary Christians, even those who live in close union
with God, there is as vast a difference as between talent
and genius. In this matter we may make our own, with
some reservations, the thought expressed by Léon Bloy:

"No one seems to realize that sanctity is a supernatural gift which differentiates one man from another
just as if their very natures were changed. Nor does this
come about either suddenly or little by little. It is a something which occurs in the profundity of God, in the silent
depths of His Will. The saint, like the genius, is a man
apart, as lonely, as solitary, as alone of his kind as would
be a plant that might have strayed down to us from the
Garden of Eden. There is no road leading from talent to
genius; so vast is the distance between the highest peak of
virtue and the lowest valley of sanctity that all the
torrents of the universe could flow unhindered in the vast
intervening space."

A true saint is an incomparable gift of God. It would be
reward enough for a parish, a diocese, or a country, if it
succeeded in producing one such élite soul. The worth-
while people in life are the great men — the saints. Omit
a few men of genius, and the face of history is changed.
The same holds true with the saints. The profound influence of Brother André, both during his life and after his
death, is a proof of this; what really matters to God is not

so much the number as the quality of his apostles and faithful. Though our lives may not show marked spiritual superiority and genius, they must nevertheless be deeply impregnated with the supernatural. The carvings sculptured on the bronze portals of medieval cathedrals by the pupils of great masters, while expressive of much Christian beauty, cannot compare with the ravishing works of the artists themselves; so in our lives: though we cannot equal the perfection of the canonized saints, we must endeavor to resemble them, and carve on our souls the image of Christ our Master.

THE PERSONALITIES
OF TWO HOLY MEN

ALL saints show a striking similarity to one another because of the fact that their conduct is modelled on that of Christ and their inner life is a reproduction of His Gospel. Besides this fundamental resemblance, certain ones of them present other identical traits of beauty, just as the works of two disciples of a great artist may reflect the same characteristic inspiration of their master.

When we attentively consider Brother André's face, we instinctively draw a parallel between him and Jean-Marie Vianney. The French sculptor, Vermare, who had made a statue of that Saint, when introduced to Brother André, was so impressed by his likeness to the face he had attempted to carve, that he exclaimed enthusiastically: "My Curé of Ars, my Curé of Ars. . . . What a remarkable face! What expression in his eyes! How I would like to mould that head!"

Brother André struck this artist who had carefully studied the features of the Curé of Ars as being a counterpart of that Saint. His outward appearance manifested the same holiness. Everyone knows how much one's intellectual or spiritual life stamps itself on the countenance, and how much the eye reflects the interior flame that glows in a man's breast. Voltaire is said to have shown a striking similarity with the Curé of Ars in features, though not in his countenance. In Voltaire's face could be detected a subtle shrewdness, a sneering malignity, a cunning expression of knavery; whereas the countenance of the Curé of Ars was expressive of mildness, humility, and kindness, of guilelessness alloyed with keenness of wit, of nobility of mind and of purpose. In our two holy men the likeness is that of the soul.

The comparison of these two outstanding lives will throw a flood of light on the main features of him whose life we are studying.

★
★　★

Jean-Marie Vianney was indebted to his beloved mother for his early religious training. She had a predilection for him. "My little Jean-Marie," she often said to him, "if I should see you offending God I would feel greater sorrow than if it were another one of my children." Fondled by his mother more than were his brothers and sisters, little Alfred, who used to recite his prayers close beside her, making use of her Rosary beads, must have heard the same words. How true it is that virtue is infused from a mother's heart into the hearts of her children, who are so prone to imitation.

Both men were reared in poverty, and their youth was fraught with trials. Both met with hardships at home and difficulties in their studies.

The episode of Alfred, caught praying in the barn, reminds us of young Jean-Marie kneeling also in the stable in front of a small statue.

No less charming is the incident when both invited comrades to pray with them; these, being once caught, never returned because of the long continuance of the prayer.

Both mortified themselves and sacrificed themselves a

long time before the multitudes began coming to them. They slept on hard floors, fasted continually, deprived themselves heroically of all that is sweet in life, and prepared themselves for their mission by a life fraught with prayers and sufferings. Both were misunderstood by the authorities, and met with hostility; both had to face adversaries, even when their work was crowned with success.

In spite of their humble submission, they could not be deterred by the fiercest opposition. "When Brother André wants something," one of his confrères asserted, "obedience alone can make him change his mind."

We all know about the assaults of the devil on the poor Curé of Ars. Such encounters with the Evil One were less frequent in the case of Brother André but he, too, had some contact with him.

Before appearing to him in the form of an animal attempting to frighten him, the devil had waged many useless attacks against him; but vain had been the cunning artifices of the the Evil One against his plain, upright simplicity; vain, likewise, the diabolical attempts to dishearten him by whispering in his ear such words as, "You are surely mistaken. . . . You are going to fail and be ridiculed. . . . You will be rejected by your Congregation."

Brother André was not wont to speak willingly of his open struggles with Satan, but he frequently reminded his friends of the presence of the unclean spirit on earth and he gave them to understand that he sometimes had physical encounters with him.

We must speak of such matters with circumspection. But who would reject as fancies, facts alleged by persons of undeniable prudence, reliability, and trustworthiness? How shall we account for the strange sound which was heard when he came from his visits to the dying? In his wretched lodging under the roof of the primitive chapel

[149]

he heard frightening noises during entire nights. Once when one of his friends was sleeping there, he was awakened by a deafening tumult like the rattling of chains and the stamping of feet on the floor.

"Brother André," he exclaimed, "surely there are burglars in the chapel."

"No, do not be afraid," he answered simply, as if he were familiar with such nightly visits.

A parish priest on a pilgrimage was determined to meet Brother André. Father Superior said to him:

"Go up to his room above the chapel. He will be glad to welcome you."

The priest ascended the narrow stairway leading to the roof, but he stopped, astonished at hearing inside a noise as of someone wrestling, and dared not knock at the door.

"Go away, leave me alone! Go away!"

The priest ran to the Superior.

"Are you sure Brother André is alone in his cell?"

"I am positive of it. He retired just a few moments ago to pray and take some rest."

"Then, that noise which I just heard and which frightened me must be what I thought it was, a fight with the devil."

On many occasions Brother André declared that he was afraid to enter his room on account of a black animal which appeared to him. He reported to a confrère that one day he felt something like a hand squeezing his leg tightly.

One night, on his return from visiting the sick, he began speaking to his companion of the goodness and the power of Saint Joseph, who had erected the sanctuary on Mount Royal, showing him at the same time the work done in repairing and enlarging the presbytery. While thus talking, he stood on the threshold of a room on the ground-floor where the lateral beams were as yet only partially floored. Suddenly, he was hurled inside, a distance of about twelve feet over the uncovered beams. His legs struck the edge of an opening and he received a violent blow on the head as he fell to the ground. His bewildered companion, passing round the open space, rushed to his rescue and brought him to his room. The Brother seemed reluctant to give any account of the adventure. His friend was puzzled at the incident, since he knew it was a physical impossibility for an old man to make such a jump. The only explanation given by the Brother to his companion was the loan of the biography of a saint who was frequently transported by the devil.

Sometimes the Brother spoke confidentially of his bouts with Satan, the enemy of his works. Some will perhaps listen to such narratives with a shrug of the shoulders.

"What! You do not mean to speak of interventions of the devil in the twentieth century!"

Alas! Satan can gain no greater victory than to cause men to deny his influence in the world. An enemy has a good opportunity for harm, an easy access to those who ignore his approach. If the devil very rarely removes his mask in the presence of ordinary Christians, he does so sometimes to vent his spite against those who see through his artifices. Instances of diabolical attacks are found in the life of Christ and in the lives of the saints throughout the ages.

The apostle of Saint Joseph did not allow himself to be troubled at these vexations, because he considered them as a sign that good had been accomplished or was about to be accomplished. He could have repeated the words of the Curé of Ars: "The devil is angry — so much the better! How stupid he is; he is just announcing the coming of great sinners to me!"

These two great, apostolic souls knew no greater suffering than to behold the hardness of men's hearts. Referring to the numerous miracles performed at the Oratory, Brother André remarked:

"Miracles are wrought that the world may open its eyes and be converted, but it seems as if it were blind."

Very often he wept over Communism.

Amid the success of his apostolate, he occasionally met with incredible resistance. A man addicted to drunkenness and debauchery promised him one day that he would amend.

"If you heal that person," he declared in the presence of a man whose leg was in a state of putrefaction, "no Christian will be more fervent than I."

Shortly after, the request was granted, but the man refused to yield to evidence, cynically denying the supernatural nature of the cure. The Brother did not lose hope and said to him later:

"If I free you from your craving for forbidden pleasures, will you be converted?"

"Do not do that," came the cynical answer. "You need not go to so much trouble. God has His angels; He has no need of me."

Like the Curé of Ars, Brother André was taxed with insanity; he was the object of hideous slanders: his enemies made him a target for their shafts.

Our two saintly men used an identical program of life: long office hours interrupted by hours of prayer on the Brother's part; for the priest, his Breviary, prayer, and endless hours in the confessional. They took the same recreation, visiting the sick. The humble country pastor attracted crowds by the fascination of his holiness; the poor college porter worked the same marvel in the same unobtrusive way.

Both kept a smiling humility amid the chorus of praise called forth by their charitable deeds. Brother André, too, saw bishops kneeling at his feet, a fact which nevertheless did not prevent him from styling himself the little servant of Saint Joseph, nor deter him from begging prayers for his own conversion.

Each had a modest opinion of himself. Both were solicitous that God, the Author of all good, should not be robbed of His glory. How indignant was Brother André when he met persons who placed all their confidence in him and neglected to have recourse to God in prayer!

Both were intent on concealing their good deeds by introducing into the conversation a pun or an appropriate joke.

There exists a difference between them, however, in their manner toward those who tried to obtain their relics. The Curé of Ars laughed at such veneration and sold, at a high price, his clothes, his hair, even the last tooth in his mouth, to raise alms. Brother André remained intractable in this respect and was unsparing in his rebukes to those whom he suspected of such designs. A motive of virtue inspired each of these opposite lines of conduct: the one was prompted by charity, the other by humility.

It may be said of the Curé of Ars that his theology is summed up in the first and greatest of commandments: the world, created and redeemed by divine love, is saved by rising to the love of God. Such was also the summary of Brother André's teaching. They both scorned eloquence and were ignorant of it; they had a simple manner of speech which went straight to the heart.

"Do you love God?" Brother André asked a visitor.

"Yes," was the somewhat hesitant answer.

"What signs of love do you give Him? How often, for

instance, do you receive Holy Communion? Once a week? Once a month?"

"Once in a while. Is that not sufficient?"

"When you have an intimate friend, do you let whole weeks, whole months go by without going to see him, without giving him tokens of affection, not knowing what to say to him? What sacrifices do you make for Jesus, Who died on the Cross for our salvation? Ah! If we only really loved God!"

Tears flowed down his withered old cheeks.

Even strangers were deeply moved by such words and tears and many proclaimed that they were indebted to him for their conversion. For example:

"I had come to petition a favor: Brother André spoke to me of the love of God in such a touching manner that I completely changed my ideas on religion. I realized that one can live for years in the state of mortal sin almost unaware. He made me understand my obligations as a Christian, and now I receive Communion daily and I try to make God loved by those about me."

Brother André worked conversions among well-known Freemasons, Jews, and Protestants. Though he was reserved on the subject of miracles, he delighted in describing the art of preparing the way for grace in the soul.

From his innumerable conversions we may cite the following: A former pupil of Notre Dame College had ceased to practise his religion for about twenty years. Then he fell grievously ill. He resisted all the entreaties of his family, who tried in vain to obtain his deathbed conversion. In their despair they had recourse to Brother André. The latter contrived the following scheme to ensnare the sinner:

"Since he does not want to see a priest, speak to him about his classmates, his professors, and the former college porter. Ask him if he would like to see me," he told them.

The scheme succeeded and the Brother was sent for.

"You must prepare yourself to die," he whispered to him. "You must not be afraid of Jesus. He forgave the good thief, who was not less guilty than you." Then he spoke to him about the mercy of God and described the Passion, adding: "It is not too late, send for a priest. Take this medal of Saint Joseph."

The patient began to weep and promised to receive any confessor Brother André should choose to send him. The Brother whispered to the one whom he entrusted with this duty:

"Make it easy for him: do not scold him."

To win souls, Brother André, like the Curé of Ars, relied on Him Who chose to make use of the simple words he uttered. The secrets of the heart were revealed to him. Before recommending a novena he told some to go to confession, but with others he omitted this injunction, knowing that they lived as good Christians.

A stranger who came to ask a cure was thus addressed:

"Why did you let hogs into your house? Go first to cleanse your soul, go to confession."

Referring to a stranger, he declared: "That man's prayer will not be heard because he did not come with proper dispositions."

One day, one of Brother André's intimate friends saw a blind man sobbing out loud in the primitive chapel near the crypt. He went to him and whispered:

"You must have confidence, my friend."

"I am blind, and I have come from a great distance to ask to be cured."

"Have you seen Brother André?"

"Yes, He told me to go to the church to pray. I went,

but my prayer remains unanswered."

"Go back to see him."

The blind man complied, but soon returned without obtaining his petition.

Brother André's friend then went to his office: "So your blind man will go back home without being cured?"

"Do you know him?"

"No. He is a stranger. I saw him weeping and I went to speak to him."

"He will not be cured so long as he lives with another man's wife."

"Did he tell you that?"

"There is no danger of his telling it."

Without noticing it, he was revealing his power of reading the inmost secrets of the heart.

A young lady came to Father Superior and said:

"My brother wants to get married. We are five daughters, our parents are dead, my brother is our sole support. Pray to Saint Joseph that he may change his mind."

"Go to see Brother André."

She complied, but she would not tell everything.

"I came to ask for prayers."

"For what intentions?"

"For my intentions."

When she had gone, Brother André remarked: "How nonsensical to use such secrecy! She came to ask me to pray for her intentions but her intentions are not good. Her brother is not going to spoil his future on her account; he has a right to get married."

If the Brother rebuked certain importunate visitors, Saint John Vianney did not act otherwise. Ladies were often coldly received by each of them, but sinners alway received a hearty welcome.

As instances of this fact here are two scenes sketched from life. The Brother was talking with a friend in his office. A lady came in and began speaking with volubility of her ailings. In vain did the Brother try to interject a few words.

"If you do not want me to talk," he said, "go and settle things with God."

She went out, and the Brother said to his friend:

"If she can bear that patiently, she deserves to obtain her request."

A woman suffering from severe inflammatory rheumatism for several years came up.

"Brother André, I am very ill."

"No, you are not."

"Why, yes, I have come to obtain relief."

"I tell you that you are not sick," came the Brother's sharp answer.

Disconcerted and intimidated, the woman dared not insist and went away.

"I should have held my own," she thought to herself. But from that moment she felt no further attack of the suffering which had formerly kept her in bed for weeks at a time.

Like the Curé of Ars, Brother André always showed himself a stern opponent of indecent styles and immodest attire.

The former openly expressed his joy at the death of a young child, saying:

"Happy mother! Happy son, for whom the time of trial has been shortened!"

The latter, it is true, often cured infants, but he sometimes declared to parents who besought him in tears to heal their child:

"You don't know what the future has in store for him:

[157]

he will perhaps be a cause of grief to you and you will wish that he had died and gone to Heaven. If he gets well, I do not want to be responsible for the future."

Brother André and Saint John Vianney displayed the same supernatural prudence in their counsels to the thousands of people who sought their advice.

To these similarities in their work with souls, may be added many others pertaining to their inner lives.

They constantly meditated on the Passion of our Divine Lord and described it in the same manner. Both were remarkable for their spirit of prayer, their continual union with God in the midst of all-absorbing occupations and cares.

The Curé of Ars was fond of describing Heaven and used to shed tears as he exclaimed: "We shall see it! We shall see it!" Brother André also seemed to anticipate heavenly bliss and could not refrain from weeping when he spoke of it. He begged of God that his attitude towards Him might be that of the blessed in Heaven.

Both were penetrated with this truth: our earthly existence must be looked upon merely as a preparation for the next life and as a prerequisite for admittance to that blissful abode. In their estimation, our present life should be an anticipated paradise. They seemed to be strangers to this earth and considered themselves as citizens of the eternal country only. To use the expression of the Thomists, they espoused the customs and manners of the Deity by their conformity to the spirit of Christ.

Much more could be said to complete the parallel between these two saintly figures. Neither was entirely free from imperfections, but these serve to show the divine action more obviously. The picturesque definition of a saint by the Curé of Ars may well be applied to both: "A little skin on an armful of bones." Both were lacking in vigor, both were small in stature, both were humble in deportment. They both mastered but one science, that of Jesus, and Him Crucified.

God is so jealous of His own glory that He selects the most humble as His instruments; He commissions them to seek the lost sheep, to dress bleeding wounds, to heal bodies, and to give solace and repentance to souls. Throughout the ages history repeats itself, the history of the humble Galilean fishermen sent to conquer the world.

XIII

LAST DAYS ON EARTH

WE HAVE sketched the career and life work of one who was like another Curé of Ars. We shall now contemplate him at the close of his earthly existence. With the emaciated face of an ascetic, with small subdued eyes shining brightly and with an habitual smile he still seemed young and alert. His voice had become shrill and tremulous with the advancing years. His energetic attempts to hold himself erect made him appear younger than his years.

During the last year of his life, the venerable nonagenarian could not receive visitors regularly. In his intermittent visits at the Oratory we noticed with sorrow that his strength was rapidly weakening. On Wednesdays and Sundays only could he go to his Bureau.

"I am going to my 'Bourreau,'" he would laughingly say. (Bourreau means tormentor, executioner.)

"Another day in Purgatory," he would say with a smile, after receiving the people for hours.

During the summer he spent several days resting with relatives and friends. To these charitable people who had the good fortune of affording him an oasis of peace and tranquillity, he delighted in describing the beauties of Heaven.

His untiring zeal urged him to consume all his remaining strength in doing good to his neighbor. Once, on returning from a sick call, he almost collapsed and had to be supported by the one who accompanied him. He frequently had violent heart attacks; but as soon as he felt relieved he was ready to continue his work of curing bodies and converting souls.

His superiors, who saw him fast declining, wished him to see, before his death, the dream of his life realized, the completion of the basilica; but proceedings undertaken for that purpose seemed to be of no avail. An act of faith removed all difficulties. At the meeting of the Council at the Oratory the first Wednesday of November, 1935, good Brother André suggested that a statue of Saint Joseph be placed within the unfinished walls of the basilica. That same day after dinner we went to the primitive shrine to pray for a moment and then we climbed the steep hill to the basilica. Brother André tried to follow the procession but, exhausted with fatigue, had to stop. With a mournful sadness, a painful anguish of heart while performing this act of faith, we all had the same presentiment; the basilica will be completed, but its artisan, Brother André, will not enjoy his triumph on earth. Going up the rugged concrete stairway, we reached the spacious nave with its enormous pillars; here and there we could catch a glimpse of the sky through the scaffolding.

The statue of Saint Joseph was placed in the apse. As we recited the prayers, we were overwhelmed by the greatness of the work accomplished on Mount Royal. It seemed evident that the venerable man was really inspired from above when he proposed to take this step, which was a repetition of the gesture of faith made by him forty years earlier, when he had placed a small statue in a crevice of the rock. By this same confidence, the work of the Oratory was to be continued. All the obstacles which had seemed insurmountable were removed. The required permission were granted, a loan was raised, and a great master w chosen to replace the deceased architect and to retouch his plans.

The aged Brother insisted on getting permission to make his annual trip to the United States. He wished to see his American friends once more and hoped to collect the offerings needed to carry on the construction of the church.

When he returned, he appeared to be feeling better and to be full of courage and joy. On the night of his arrival he stole into the darkness of the crypt, and there he placed as votive offerings, the crutches and instruments of suffering discarded by those whom he had healed during his journey.

Yet he seemed to have a presentiment of his coming death. Already in October he had said to Mr. Chartier, who was sculpturing his bust: "It is certain that the basilica will be continued; I am useless now — it is time for me to go."

A few days before Christmas a confrère said to him: "The people were right in saying that you would live to see your basilica."

"I never said I would see it finished."

As a rule, God's servants do not live to see their work completed. Would our Brother André be an exception to this rule? In spite of gloomy forebodings it was still hoped that he would live to see the basilica open to worship.

At the midnight Mass he was there in his stall behind the altar, kneeling all the time, his head in his hands, lost in adoration. Fatigue compelled him to retire before the end of the third Mass. His face was bright with joy. Very probably he was thinking: "Within a year or two the feast of Christmas will be celebrated in the basilica." To his lips came his *Nunc Dimittis.* On his way to his room he said to the Father who accompanied him: "I have done all I had to do; the work has no need of me now."

That night at supper an old friend who had clung to him

since the very beginning of the Oratory said:

"Another Christmas day is coming to a close."

"It is probably my last."

"But, the Oratory still needs you."

"If one can do good on earth, he can do far more in Heaven."

The next day, as he was coming homeward in a car with a friend, he passed near the little hospital at Saint-Laurent, where he was to die. Looking at it, he said: "What a fine place to rest! What a fine place for patients to prepare for death!"

Yet he had never stayed there.

That same night, December 26, 1936, he was stricken with an attack of acute gastritis, the illness which was to bring on his death. In the evening of the thirty-first, he was rushed to the hospital at Saint-Laurent. At the moment of his departure from the monastery, pale and trembling as he was, lying on a stretcher, he still had the courage to smile and to say to the interns who wrapped him up carefully: "I look like a man leaving for the North Pole." At the hospital, after a violent attack of pain, he confided to the nursing Sister: "The Great Almighty is coming."

He still had three days to wait for the meeting with the Beloved — three days of suffering, which he supported with his usual genial smile.

"Why don't you ask Saint Joseph to heal you?" someone asked him.

And he who had restored health to so many replied: "I can do nothing for myself."

He retained to the end his lucidity of mind and his smiling gayety. Grateful for the least service rendered him and forgetful of his sufferings, he cheerfully received al' those who came to see him. When he summoned a nun to his bedside, smiling, he said by way of excuse: "It is your old nuisance who is ringing again."

His paralyzed arm caused him very severe pains.

"My arm," he said, "is a Communist; the wicked thing hates me!"

"Are you suffering much?" someone inquired.

"Indeed I am, but I thank God for giving me the grace to suffer; I need it so much!"

He practised perfectly to the very end the doctrine of suffering accepted with gratitude, a doctrine which he had preached during his whole life. A few years before, his aged sister, when sick, had said to him: "Do heal me, you know how much I am suffering; you cure everybody and yet you will not do anything for me!"

"It is not I who heals, it is Saint Joseph. But suffer and accept everything for God's sake. It is better for us to suffer before death."

Stretched upon his bed of pain, the good Brother said to his superior: "Father, we do not think enough about death. I have something to ask of you: pray for my conversion."

Thus he accepted death for the expiation of his sins, but to that intention he seemed to join another of capital importance. His constant inquiries about the illness of the Pope, and his stressing of how little importance he was in the world compared to the great Pontiff, lead us to conjecture that the little old man of Mount Royal gave up his life for the venerable old man of the Eternal City.

"Does the Holy Father still suffer much?" he often inquired.

A few days previously he confessed to friends who were telling him how much the Oratory still needed his services: "There is one who is far more necessary than Brother André in this world: that is the Pope. If the Holy Father passed away, it would be a disaster; he still has much to accomplish."

He also offered his prayers and sufferings for the intentions of bloodstained Spain, and he inquired several times about the fratricidal war that was being waged in that country.

Until his death he was preoccupied about the completion of the Oratory; but he still maintained the most unalterable confidence. Twice he asserted in unmistakable words, after being informed of the steps taken by the superiors in regard to the continuation of the work: "We shall succeed; the temple to Saint Joseph will be completed."

On January 4, 1937, about eleven o'clock in the evening, in the midst of his intolerable pain he spoke about the work on Mount Royal:

"You cannot realize all the good God accomplishes at the Oratory. What misfortunes there are in the world! I was in a position to know. I had need of being everything: lawyer, doctor, priest; but God was helping me. How powerful He is!"

He related how Saint Joseph used to heal the sick, how a certain paralytic was cured and was able to walk with him and accompany him to the Benediction of the Blessed Sacrament; how another one was sent to confession.

"How good God is! How beautiful, how powerful! He must indeed be beautiful since the soul, which is but a ray of His beauty, is so beautiful!"

Just before succumbing to the final phase of his illness, he murmured: "O Mary, my sweet Mother, Mother of my sweet Saviour, be merciful to me and assist me."

Then faintly, "Saint Joseph" — his further words became unintelligible.

During the three hours before he fell into a state of coma, he kept repeating that complaint full of resignation "My God, how greatly am I suffering!"

Then began the great silence which preceded his death and lasted more than twenty hours. On the morning of the fifth, about eight o'clock, he received Extreme Unction in the presence of many friends and confrères who were watching the awful agony.

As he was rapidly declining, the nuns ceased to refuse admittance to the people who had discovered his place of refuge. All day long until his death there was an uninterrupted flow of visitors to his bedside, all showing deepest love and veneration. For forty years Brother André had been receiving the sick. On his deathbed, he still continued to do so.

Each one approached with respect and in profound silence, bringing some religious article to touch his bloodless, emaciated hands, those old hands which had rubbed and healed so many sick persons. His confrères, with tearful eyes, took off the crucifixes and medals worn on their religious habit to touch his body. Brother André, with his eyes closed, seemed to have fallen asleep. Men, young and old, women, small children, all approached. While their lips murmured a prayer, their eyes bespoke the fervor of their desire: "Good Brother André," was their silent supplication, "when you are in Heaven, remember us."

In many homes, on that eve of the Epiphany, the usual rejoicings of the festive season were cast aside. All were listening on the radio, to hear the latest news on the condition of the aged Brother dying in the little hospital. Entire families were on their knees. "Saint Joseph, save our Brother André. He healed my father, my mother, my sister, my little brother, my friend — he healed me."

It was as if a member of the family were in the throes of death. The dying man was the friend, the benefactor of all. Thousands of signal favors had been granted through his intercession.

In the sick room a few confrères were kneeling in ardent

supplication. Behind the crypt, at the shrine, workmen were hurriedly preparing the tomb, and the blows of the hammers resounded, cavernous, amplified and re-echoed by the mountain. We still clung to a last ray of hope: "He will not die, he must not die, he must see his basilica finished." Those thoughts assailed us in the midst of our occupations, while the image of the dying religious was constantly present to our mind. As soon as we could spare a moment, we repaired to his bedside. Alas! the progress of the malady was becoming more alarming.

"He has only a few hours to live," the doctors declared.

Those who saw him then, during that long period of silence, remembered a scene which had taken place four years before. At that time Brother André had double pneumonia and seemed at the point of death.

One night the patient had been left alone. An intimate friend, resting in an adjoining room in case of need, heard the Brother call. He ran quickly to the sick room, where Brother André, quite upset, painfully told his trouble: "I think I was dreaming, though I am not sure. The devil was holding me by the neck and was almost choking me. I feel very ill; I have a pain in my heart. Do you know that one can desire death in order to be with God!"

At his request his attendant rubbed his chest with the medal of Saint Joseph, and to distract him said: "I think it is permitted, but there is no hurry, we still need you. I saw Heaven in a dream, Brother André."

And he began to describe the dazzling beauty of God, the splendor of the angels, the elect, the Blessed Virgin and Saint Joseph, somewhat in the manner in which Brother André had often spoken about it: "Near Saint Joseph," he said, "there was a fine armchair. Approaching, I asked boldly for whom this fine seat was reserved."

" 'For my best friend on earth,' " replied Saint Joseph.

" 'Do you not fear another will occupy it?' "

" 'No, I have engraved his name on it. Look at it closely.' "

"Guess what I read, Brother?"

Brother André, who had listened to the tale with interest, without suspecting the hidden snare, said: "What was it?"

"I read 'Brother André.' "

"Oh, don't say that; I wish only to be Saint Joseph's little dog."

"Yes, but that little dog will bark so loud that the whole world will hear it."

While recalling this episode, we still clung to a last ray of hope: if only God would will to leave Brother André with us! If only He would let him continue his life of loving goodness!

Some friends and his confrères from the Oratory spent the evening by his bedside. In spite of our hopes, the patient was becoming more and more feeble.

By now this critical condition had lasted almost twenty hours. About half past eleven, all were quickly called in, for his respiration seemed to have stopped. The final, consoling prayers, the litany for the dying, and that of Saint Joseph were recited.

The patient became calm once more, his breathing more regular. Will God spare our dear Brother André? Vain hope! Once again his breathing became very difficult. Half past twelve brought the last agony.

Ardent prayers again rose to Heaven. Then, at fifty minutes past midnight on Wednesday, January 6, 1937, Brother André died.

The *De Profundis* did not express our thought; the words of the *Magnificat* rose unconsciously to our lips.

We contemplated the face which had recovered its calm in death, and we intoned the very hymn which God's chosen one must have sung on his entrance into Heaven, the *Te Deum*, the while we seemed to hear the words of Jesus to His faithful servant:

"Come, ye blessed of My Father, . . . for I was sick, and you visited Me."

"But when, O Lord, did I see Thee sick and come to Thee?"

"Amen, I say to you, as long as you did it to one of these My least brethren, you did it to Me."

XIV

TRIUMPH

THE Feast of the Epiphany, January 6, 1937, the day commemorating Our Saviour's Manifestation, was the day chosen for the exaltation of His faithful imitator, Brother André; it was also the first Wednesday of the new year to be dedicated to Saint Joseph.

"Brother André is dead! Brother André is dead!" The sorrowful exclamation reverberated in every home and was echoed all over the American continent, and farther. Even Protestants and agnostics had a passing thought for the aged Brother who had just died in the obscure hospital at Saint-Laurent.

The mortuary mask was moulded; the extraction of the heart was performed. Out of respect the body was not embalmed, though it was to be exposed for a whole week to the veneration of the faithful. Already visitors began to throng. During the cold and dreary afternoon, the body was taken to the Oratory, followed by a crowd of confrères and friends, while the bells of the church and the College of Saint-Laurent tolled his passing.

As the funeral procession approached Mount Royal it became a triumph. The crowd descended the hill to meet their great friend and joined in the procession for the solemn entrance into the crypt of the Oratory. The remains of Brother André were placed in a lateral chapel opposite the main entrance of the church built at the cost of his many sacrifices.

There, in an atmosphere of Paradise, the whole crowd sang the *Magnificat* in front of the tomb, and when Father Albert Cousineau, the Superior of the Oratory, summed up, in a voice trembling with emotion, the life-work of Brother André and recalled his last moments, there were audible sobs and smothered weeping.

Around the poor coffin of plain wood covered with black cloth, the faithful pressed forward in crowds which could hardly be controlled. For a whole week they were to throng there without interruption. Letters of sympathy, telegrams from bishops and notables, came in profusion to the Oratory. Religious Communities took part in the mourning. Many columns were written on the departed one in nearly every newspaper of America, written in every language and by men of all creeds. It was more than a national mourning.

In spite of inclement weather, of melting snow, rain, and the ice which covered the pavement, visitors swarmed to Mount Royal. There was a continual procession in front of the tomb. All wished to have a last glance at the great friend of the people; they wished to touch his remains with medals, beads, crucifixes. Late in the evening the crowds dispersed, but the doors of the church remained open all night long.

*
*   *

On Saturday, January the ninth, under a chilly downpour of rain, the crowd walked through the streets, following the remains, which were conveyed to the Montreal Cathedral. The vast edifice was found too small to hold the multitudes.

The *Requiem* was impregnated with a restrained joy; yes, more — the triumph of the *Resurrexit*, the flight of a prayer already heard; it was dominated with the thought of the eternal light, the unending rest enjoyed by the departed one.

When the last liturgical prayer was said, the people filed past to venerate the remains. Outside, a strong wind scattered the clouds in every direction. Once more men, women and children formed a procession. In spite of the violent gusts of wind they trudged on, irresistibly drawn in the train of the meek old man who had loved them so much. They plodded through the hilly streets, heedless of the weather, to the Oratory, where for the past thirty-three years, they had been attracted by his goodness and love.

Before the ascent of the mountain, a short halt was made at Notre Dame College. The coffin was opened and placed in the very spot where, during forty years, Brother André had exercised the humble functions of porter. And there around the coffin gathered the old, grey-haired confrères who had lived with him during his hidden life. One of these had helped him to trace the first pathway up the mountain; another, a living image of Saint Joseph, now hoary with old age, had helped to erect the first shrine; a third had been Brother André's consolation during the sorrowful hours of his great trial. They all stood round, recalling scenes of the long ago, proud of their former companion in arms. One by one the college boys, representative of the generations of school children who knew Brother André as a porter, came to touch respectfully the mortal remains.

For the last time the holy religious was carried up the hill. Our memories recalled the numberless times he had travelled that road after visiting the sick, working cures, enkindling repentance, hearing human woes tearfully told to him. Now all was silent in the eternal peace, the great everlasting repose, and the remembrance of countless charitable deeds done in behalf of his fellow mortals.

He was again laid in state, with tapers burning around

his coffin opposite the main entrance in the midst of the many ex-votos left there by those whom he had healed. The uninterrupted procession of pilgrims became more and more dense.

On Sunday, it looked as if the mountain were being assaulted. All cars in Montreal seemed to have but one destination, the Oratory. Railway trains from all parts of Canada and the United States were bringing thousands who came to see for the last time the apostle of Saint Joseph. In no time, there were nearly a hundred thousand on the church grounds. The large esplanade was transformed into a field of closely packed human beings resembling a field of thickly-sown wheat; the mountain-side had become a forest of sheaves, thick-set and upright, bound together in one sheaf.

The unprecedented triumph around the body lasted day and night without stop until Tuesday. They stood there waiting their turn, four, five, or six hours, in order to have the privilege of touching for one second the feet of the deceased. Outside, the throng seemed to be at a standstill in an apparently unprogressing movement before the human ebb-tide; and yet in the interior of the church, the people filed off, two by two, in front of the coffin, at the rate of about one hundred to one hundred and twenty per minute. Cripples, blind people, and all categories of sick were carried — even a dying man was brought in on a stretcher. The throng prayed aloud or uttered enthusiastic cries when a miracle was wrought.

And the apotheosis continued in a manner utterly beyond description. Posterity can but believe this reality to be legendary. The prophecy of His Exc. Archbishop Gauthier was fulfilled. An illustrious visitor from France had once asked him: "Who is this Brother André of whom everybody is speaking?"

"He is a man of God. At his death, we shall behold more

[174]

than half of the population of Montreal hastening to his tomb."

Even very celebrated saints did not win such a triumph before their remains had scarcely grown cold. The honor and glory accorded to them seemed to be eclipsed by that shown at the death of this most humble man. A powerful blast seemed to blow over the city, which became like a stormy sea whose waves dashed against the Mount Royal hillside, so strong was the conviction that Brother André was a saint. He was accorded as much veneration and as many marks of respect as if he had already been canonized.

How many now bewail their indifference toward him, how many regret having come in contact with him without knowing it, and mourn for having possessed such a rich treasure to appreciate it only at the moment of its loss!

The story of holy men, those faithful copies of Jesus, always resembles the life of the Master. Ordinarily disowned by their kindred, their relatives, though sometimes held in great esteem by the people, they are often unrecognized and despised by a group of the envious — successors to the Pharisees and Sadducees. Thus Saint Thérèse was unappreciated in her own cloister; Saint Bernadette was looked upon as one given to hallucinations, and apparently underestimated even during her religious life; but after their death, God Himself manifested their glory to the world.

The simple and humble of heart recognize sanctity, as was the case during the life of Christ. The day of Brother André's death, the admiration hitherto withheld by the so-called intellectuals became manifest; they were led away by the popular current. Such was the case of a journalist, who frankly confessed: "I was of the number of those who thought themselves too intelligent to give credence to Brother André. And now if I had not gone to his tomb, I would regret it all my life."

[175]

The seed sown in souls by the example of Brother André is now flowering. It is not in vain that he prayed and suffered, that he faced all kinds of opposition and misunderstanding, that he was embittered against the false and self-interested piety of the people, that he offered himself as a victim, or that he desired to suffer martyrdom rather than see his people given over to the barbarity of Communism. His triumph is a guarantee of his mission. Throughout Canada and the United States he was God's sower, and the multitude of conversions among those who visit his tomb adds to the lustre of his work.

Many who had come through no other motive than idle curiosity or to follow the crowd were deeply moved. They realized suddenly that their lives were out of harmony with the sublimity of the Christian vocation. Many obdurate hearts closed to grace made their peace with God and began to love Him. In the darkness of the confessionals where grace ever awaits the repentant soul, were many avowals of sin, many moral regenerations, not only at the Oratory, but in all the churches of the city.

Only the sight of this apotheosis could give us a true idea of it. One would have to live those frenzied hours, to hear the clamor of the crowd waiting their long-deferred turn to see him, to be impelled by the irresistible impulse of their faith. We recall that spectacle with eyes brimful of tears and hearts aching and throbbing with emotion.

Such a homage to sanctity is an unconscious avowal of our hearts, which are made, not for the half-hearted faith of an anaemic religion, but for a total, absolute self-surrender, an all-sacrificing love of God. Desire for perfection is instinctive in human souls. It is found in the hearts of pagans, even in the hearts of those in whom hatred of suffering attempts to stifle that craving. The great obstacle to the extension of the reign of Christ is the want of energy among innumerable semi-Christians who, by their emasculated form of religion, give an incomplete idea of the religion of Christ. Christianity in all its beauty, its splendor, its sacrifices, is the only religion that conquers. We must judge it by its fruits, by the lives of those who conform to its Gospel. Many would be saved, when on the verge of apostasy, if they judged thus. Brother Andrés are legion in the history of the Church. In the words of a famous convert: "When we say that the Church has received eternal promises, this means there will always be saints."

The hope of the day of temporal enjoyments, of carnal enjoyments in peace and love — that dream so dear to Communists of good faith — replaces the desire to sacrifice oneself for a great cause and for a supreme happiness. Brother André lived constantly for the eternal day of infinite bliss, the only one capable of satisfying our hearts, haunted by the craving for everlasting happiness.

On Tuesday morning, a few minutes before the funeral service, the body was taken from the church through the main door for the benefit of those who were unable to enter. In the church, which on this occasion had very little of the customary funeral adornment, the Office of the Dead began. One would have liked to see the ceremonies carried out with the white vestments and floral decorations used for the saints. Bishop Limoges, of Mont-Laurier, officiated. Cardinal Villeneuve, Archbishop of Quebec, before chanting the Absolution, expressed in an inspiring panegyric the unprecedented triumph of the servant of God: "Whatever be the reputation of her children for virtue, the Church requires that, at their funeral services, prayers be said and supplications be made for the human frailties in their lives. She forbids us to anticipate the judgment which she reserves to herself, upon the heroicity of their virtues and the certainty of their entrance into Heaven. With all respect to Holy Church, however, we may say that today we celebrate the feast of humility.

"On the tomb which guards the mortal remains of this virtuous Apostle of Saint Joseph, Brother André, we may read these three words: *'Pauper, Servus, Humilis': Pauper*, that is to say, 'poor,' the religious that we so often came to see at the Oratory; *Servus*, servant, the coadjutor-Brother, the last in rank in his Community; *Humilis*, so little in his own eyes, without any suspicion of the throngs his death would bring together.

"Behold one who makes us think of another poor man, Saint Joseph, whom God put at Mary's side to watch over her virginity and to protect the divinity of her Child! Behold him whom Saint Joseph chose to build this magnificent basilica, and, above all, to spread this devotion which has taken possession of our people for the last thirty years!

"From Brother André we can rise even to Christ Himself, Who came down from heaven and was made Man in the crib to save the world. Behold, today we celebrate true Christianity! We stress the doctrine of humility, for it is to humility that we have paid homage for the past week in this church, too small to hold us all.

"O you, the little ones of earth, you who suffer, you who labor, return to your tasks and to your homes with this teaching of Christianity! Compare it with other doctrines which promise you a vain paradise on earth. This death and this funeral are a great lesson of charity for you. It is the occasion, also, of the awakening of faith and confidence in eternal happiness. We pray here for this holy servant of God, and these are the sentiments which should fill our hearts.

"You are about to return to your daily toil, to your sorrow and your sufferings. Look to the life beyond and think of the seal that the Lord puts on the life of the humble. No prince of the Church or of the State could have a funeral such as this, which affects the inmost sentiments of the heart, as we can testify today. Remember Brother André's words and hear him repeating them to us still: *Ite ad Joseph.*"

A detail seemingly of little importance but in reality quite significant is that after the Absolution, the hymn *In Paradisum*, which beseeches the angels to carry the soul to Heaven, was forgotten. That was no doubt already fulfilled. The body, transported to the burial-place, which was the chapel itself where he had been exposed, was placed in a granite sarcophagus.

The people still wished to behold the features of their beloved benefactor. Two young men who had walked fifty miles for the purpose were denied that happiness.

In the afternoon, Archbishop Gauthier came to preside over the entombing. For the last time a few privileged ones had the joy of catching a glimpse of the face of our dear departed Brother.

Kneeling before the tomb which seals the remains of the little peasant of New France whom God had singled out to propagate devotion to Saint Joseph, we think of the last sleep of the little shepherdess of France, who was entrusted with a mission similar to his, gentle Bernadette Soubirous, who likewise rests within the walls of a chapel dedicated to Saint Joseph in the garden of her cloister.

Providence guided each of them in a manner widely divergent, yet very similar. Very closely does the vocation of the poor, uneducated girl of Massabielle, chosen to spread the cult of the Immaculate Conception shortly after the proclamation of that dogma, resemble that of the humble coadjutor-Brother of Holy Cross who was destined to propagate the devotion to Saint Joseph shortly after the official choice of that Saint as the Patron of the Universal Church! Artisans of a work much out of proportion to their ability, they now wear the halo crowning the success of their mission!

XV

SURVIVAL

Brother André's unprecedented triumph at his death still persists. At every hour of the day pilgrims kneel by his tomb. The faithful servant continues to receive the people, to hear their petitions and to hand them over to Saint Joseph.

He sleeps there, in a humble alcove, a recess in the wall, which in its austere grandeur reminds us of the *Loculi* of the catacombs. Gold, marble, the riches of a pretentious funeral chapel would stand in too decided a contrast to his life of self-denial, of poverty, and of humility. Only one name stands out in relief on the black velvet-like polished granite: Frère André, C.S.C.

Very touching is the deep faith of the sick, the outcasts, the distressed, kneeling at the tomb of their friend. Often they recline their foreheads on the tomb; sometimes a mother even rests her young child on it. The ardor of their prayer is seen on their lips and in their eyes fixed on God. "Grant me this cure! Convert my child! Give me employment": such are the supplications they deposit there before leaving.

Then, by means of the escalators, they repair to Brother André's Museum where touching scenes of his life and death have been faithfully reproduced. There they may venerate the heart of the saintly religious preserved in a glass receptacle enchased in a marble stele.

[181]

At "Brother André's hour," we feel how deep is the attachment of the people to their great friend. The day after the interment, a companion, who for more than fifteen years, had conducted the line of visitors to the Brother's office, begged for authorization to come with a group of friends and commemorate the death of their common friend every first Wednesday of the month by an hour's watch at his tomb. At the first meeting, there were not a mere handful, there were more than a thousand; and since then every month, during that hour, the church is overflowing.

Another sign of the veneration of the faithful is their generous co-operation in the completion of the Oratory. The number of pilgrims is increasing and the dream of the beloved founder is becoming a reality.

Scarcely ten months after the departure of the animating spirit of the Oratory, that which was looked upon by all as an intangible dream, had become a reality; the majestic dome of the basilica towered over Mount Royal. At that time, the Religious of the Shrine renewed the gesture of faith which was asked the year before by Brother André: "You wish to roof the basilica? Place a statue of Saint Joseph within the open walls and he will soon provide a shelter for himself."

On a cold autumn afternoon we walked in procession into the apse of the basilica now roofed. In the presence of some two hundred workmen on bended knee, before the small statue of Saint Joseph, the Rosary was recited, the litany of the holy Patriarch was chanted, and the glorification of Brother André was asked for.

Even the Stations of the Cross on the mountain which the Brother had so much desired were erected. A short time before his death, seized by an unusual emotion, his face animated with his thought, he confided to a friend: "How many conversions will take place at the Stations of the Cross on the mountain! I think there will be even more there than in the basilica."

A master well known for his artistic, realistic, soul-stirring landscapes, has laid out the paths along which the crowds come to relive the Passion of Our Saviour. By the artistic drafting of paths, he has skillfully disciplined the wooded hill without doing violence to the natural harmony, while he has left nature in its primitive beauty of a capricious, uncultivated bluff covered with brushwood. The visitor who chances upon these precincts may well fancy that he has blundered into some primeval park dotted with trees of varied species.

Along the sylvan road, oaks, maples, and birches are aligned as if planted there designedly. A few stone steps here and there cut the steep hill. At places the stony framework of the mountain has been denuded. Amid the carefully laid-out scenery are short narrow footpaths, at the end of which stand high wooden crosses. Year after year, these crosses are being replaced by stone statues, as the sculptor proceeds with his gigantic work.

Thus the material work of Brother André, which is a pale image of his spiritual action, is rapidly developing.

People are beginning to meditate, to understand the life of the obscure worker, the simple lay-Brother who devoted himself entirely to the service of his brethren, the poor, the sick, and the afflicted.

Death enhanced the true figure of Brother André by effacing the slight imperfections which remained in him. No one could resist the charm of his genial smile radiant with interior happiness, his face so expressive of suffering when he spoke of the Passion of his Saviour, his feature bright with joy when he spoke with such exquisite simplicity of Saint Joseph and of Heaven.

All easily discern in him the miracle man, the man who was honest and just towards all, great and small, the social benefactor, the author of a monument which attracts millions of visitors. But the reality which only the light of a lively faith can reveal is the marvellous action of the Holy Ghost in him, the ideal of the Christian life of which he is the embodiment.

Our easy method of interpreting the Master's doctrine was unknown to him; he was a convinced Christian, a man of action, alien to the routine religion practised by the many who follow the line of least resistance. He embraced the Gospel with loyalty and followed it to the letter, despising the ungenerous attitude of the crowd.

Let us see in his plain simple life centered on God, the model of what our lives would be, did we practise entirely the doctrines of the Master. His example becomes all the more striking in our century when relaxation is almost a matter of principle, when love of the world, of comfort, of wealth for the sake of enjoyment, when the headlong pursuit of pleasure, the brutishness of vain material occupations, the practical forgetfulness of God and a surface form of Christianity mark the lives of many who call themselves Christians.

His life condemns our conception of an up-to-date Christ, like the imaginary Messiah conceived by the Jews. We have made Our Lord a model who loves riches, pleasure, sports, theatres, food, and carousal. We forget about the real Saviour, scoffed at, lashed, crucified, Him to Whose form all aspirants to the heavenly kingdom must be moulded.

The high privilege of having this living flower of the Gospel before our eyes should recall to our minds those teachings which are, unfortunately for too may of us, meaningless phrases. As we think of the influence exercised by Brother André in the Church, the words of Péguy come to our minds: "A few saints take the lead, and the long train of sinners follows after: thus is Christianity formed. A few pastors walk ahead, and the immense flock follows: thus is formed the long procession of Christendom."

The life and work of Brother André create a desire which incites souls to aspire toward a greater perfection. The holiness of Christ was the attraction which drew the crowds after Him in His days in Palestine. And since His day it is the holiness of His saints, their likeness to Christ, which is the magnet drawing their numberless followers.

True, Jesus had occasionally to reproach the Jews for following him to obtain material bread. Brother André, too, had to combat this tendency in his followers to seek for material profit, and he neglected no opportunity of turning their thoughts towards God.

By visiting the places sanctified by him and by meditating on the life he led there, the faithful may find a ladder by which they can ascend to the summit of virtue. From a casual contact with such a model, they will derive lasting benefit. Christian perfection will no longer be looked upon as mere theory, for they can see it lived in a man who struggled and suffered as they are struggling and suffering, a man who lived like them and among them.

Death has only served to increase the esteem and veneration of the people for Brother André. But is there not a tendency to exaggerate his true worth? Is there not danger that the servant may supplant his master and after spending his life in establishing devotion to Saint Joseph he may now take from his patron the glory that is his due? Such fear is ungrounded. The Carpenter of Nazareth has no such puerile fear, for he alone has prepared this triumph for his valiant servant.

Moreover, even the most ignorant among the faithful

are guided by a Christian spirit; almost all the petitions placed on Brother André's tomb ask their friend to present their requests to Saint Joseph, that God may grant them such and such a blessing.

In these times when the laboring classes are influenced by a doctrine of hate more baneful than all their material troubles, Saint Joseph is presented as their guide and patron. And Brother André has been chosen as his living model to spread devotion to him in America. Does not the obscure workman, devoting himself during his life to the suffering members of Christ, resemble the Artisan of Nazareth watching over Jesus? Brother André's mission is not merely to lead workers to Joseph, but to be a replica of the Saint, to be the laborer who has modelled his life on that of his holy protector, thus preaching to the people, in a concrete manner, labor, humility, obedience, love of God, and love of our neighbor.

It is generally conceded that a great grace has come down to us, that a Christian revival is taking place since Brother André's death. One must have lived the unforgettable days at the Oratory which followed the decease of the religious, one must needs have seen the crowds which scaled the rocky cliffs of Mount Royal a hundred thousand at a time, in order to understand that living torrent of suffering which continually sweeps toward the great sanctuary. Some come to prostrate themselves before the tomb of the powerful wonder-worker, but, feeling unworthy to approach him, they go first to cast off the burden of their sins by a good confession.

The priest sometimes asks a penitent what made him come back to God, and this is generally the answer: "I came to the Oratory at Brother André's death merely to comply with a request, and I was moved more than I can tell you, Father. I want you to proclaim publicly that it is he who drew me away from sin. Good Brother André has obtained my conversion."

Thus, after his death, the humble Brother continues to fulfill the mission entrusted to him by Providence, to lead the faithful to Saint Joseph so as to bring them nearer to Jesus. The healing of souls was always the chief concern of this apostle. In the beginning of his career, he confided to a friend who was, like himself, a lay-Brother: "Ah! if I only had a priest here to purify the souls of these people who come to see me! They return with good dispositions, but who knows if they will go to confession?"

God still leaves with his servant the same power — the granting of temporal blessings through the intercession of Saint Joseph, in order to attract them and save their souls. At his tomb are renewed the marvels of which the walls of his office were witnesses.

Considering the favors obtained, the conversions and blessings ascribed to Brother André, it seems obvious that he is destined to become officially, what he already is in the hearts of the people, the saint who, with Saint Joseph, the Patron Saint of Canada, directs our nation towards its destiny.

Our sketch is coming to a close. It resembles a mosaic made by the inlaying of details selected from his long existence. We have made no attempt to cast Brother André in a ready-made mould according to a preconceived ideal of perfection; but we have delved into the secrets of his life. Our efforts have been to describe him as he was, with his limited degree of culture, and with the frailties common to human nature. We cannot fail to see that he was marked out by the Master for higher things from the first faltering steps of his childhood to the marvellously preserved strength of his advanced age.

The dearth of written documents, his own reserved and reticent nature, the secrets of his soul jealously hidden from the eyes of the world, explain the incomplete accounts

[187]

given in these pages. He shunned any incursion into his
intimate self; only a very charitable motive could impel
him from time to time to disclose the beauty of his supernatural gifts. We have purposely omitted unnecessary
names and dates and have avoided a learned critical
analysis of Brother André's life.

Just as the portrait painter in delineating the countenance selects only those details which reflect the beauty of
the soul, so we have pointed only to the highlights in the
story of this greatly favored client of Saint Joseph. These
pages, in the disarray of their hasty germination, do not
aim at describing the growth of his earthly existence, but
rather at depicting his hidden spiritual life.

The author wishes to acknowledge his indebtedness to
the confrères and intimate friends of Brother André who
helped him to penetrate into the Wonder-Worker's great
soul, and in an especial manner to the Reverend A. Mont-
plaisir, C.S.C., a talented guide and critic.

This work is intended as a token of faithful loyalty to
the memory of our dear departed Brother. In a gesture of
love, we come to deposit it on his tomb amid the many
tributes placed there by unknown hands.

Good Brother André, having learned to know you better,
we penetrate into the crypt with its surbased vault and
stained-glass windows sparing of light, and there, lost in
the crowd of pilgrims, we kneel at your tomb. You still
remain the vital power of the Oratory. In the minds of the
people you are still very much alive; you are still the old
man, white with age, so pale and yet ever kind and smiling,
the frail old man with the eyes of youth.

In your lifetime visitors always asked where they could
find Brother André. Today, the same question is asked,
and the guide directs them to your tomb. The contact
with the cold marble which encloses your mortal remains
continues the wonderful action of your emaciated hands.

[188]

From heaven you shower your favors. You remain the intermediary agent between us and Saint Joseph. Your words: "The good one does on earth is nothing in comparison with what he will be able to do in Heaven," are an echo of the promise made by little Thérèse of Lisieux: "I want to spend my eternity doing good on earth."

We fervently beg you to hear our prayer which summarizes your life:

"O Jesus, Thou who hast wished, through the efforts of Brother André, to propagate devotion to Thy adopted father, Saint Joseph, grant that the Church may, without delay, glorify this faithful friend of the poor, the sick, and the afflicted."

Translation finished and dedicated to Brother André on Wednesday, May the Tenth, Nineteen Thirty-Eight, Octave of the Feast of Saint Joseph.

A CHRONOLOGICAL SUMMARY

Aug. 9, 1845: Birth of Alfred Bessette near the Iberville county village of St. Grégoire, about 30 miles southeast of Montreal. He was the eighth of 12 children born to Isaac Bessette and Clothilde Foisy. He was so feeble at birth that his parents decided to baptize him immediately. He was conditionally baptized the next day by Rev. Pierre A. Sylvestre, pastor of the village church.

About 1849: The Bessette family moved to Farnham.

Feb. 20, 1855: Death of Isaac Bessette, crushed under a tree. Clothilde kept her children for a time and then, exhausted, she allowed them to be put up for adoption. She went to live with her sister Rosalie, Mrs. Timothée Nadeau, at St. Césaire d'Iberville. Only Alfred, the feeblest of the children, went with her.

Nov. 20, 1857: Death of Clothilde Foisy. She was buried in Farnham. Alfred remained with Timothée Nadeau and later was adopted by the mayor of St. Césaire, Mr. Louis Ouimet.

About 1863: Alfred emigrated to the United States and worked in textile mills.

About 1867: He returned to his country as did many other French-Canadians when the Canadian Confederation became a fact. He settled at St. Césaire.

Oct. 10, 1869:   Six members of the Congregation of Holy Cross opened a school at St. Césaire.

Dec. 8, 1870:   Pope Pius IX proclaimed Saint Joseph patron of the universal Church.

Dec. 27, 1870:   Alfred Bessette became a novice in the Congregation of Holy Cross on the advice of his friend Pastor André Provençal. In receiving his religious habit, he took the name Brother André, the given name of Pastor Provençal.

Jan. 8, 1872:   The provincial council of Holy Cross decided not to admit Brother André to his religious profession. The reason: His delicate health. Yet, he was permitted to stay as a novice.

Aug. 22, 1872:   First vows of Brother André. He was officially named porter at College Notre Dame in Montreal, a position he retained until 1909.

Feb. 2, 1874:   Perpetual vows of Brother André.

May 9, 1878:   Publication of the first written testimony on the cases of five cures attributed to the prayers of Brother André. One of the cases reported dated from the previous year. Brother André then was 31 years old.

Oct. 19, 1904:   The founding of Saint Joseph's Oratory and the blessing of the first wooden chapel wich mesured 15 by 18 feet.

July 1, 1908:   Construction of a 100-foot shelter behind the wooden chapel.

Sept. 1, 1910:   Inauguration of the sacristy, the room and the chapel's new belfry.

Dec. 16, 1917:   Opening and blessing of the stone crypt.

Aug. 31, 1924:   Blessing of the cornerstone and the start of construction of the large basilica.

Jan. 6, 1937:   Death of Brother André. During seven days, a million persons passed by his bier, day and night, at the Oratory.

During 1966:   Completion of the interior of the basilica.

June 12, 1978:   Pope Paul VI declared Brother André venerable.

May 23, 1982:   Pope John Paul II beatified Brother André before a crowd of 30,000 pilgrims and visitors gathered on St. Peter's Square, at the Vatican.

June 20, 1982:   A crowd of more than 50,000 persons attended a Mass at Montreal's Olympic Stadium to celebrate the beatification of Brother André.

Sept. 11, 1984: Pope John Paul II knelt and prayed at the tomb of Blessed Brother André on the occasion of his visit to Canada.